HACKING
ENGAGEMENT
Again

HACKING ENGAGEMENT Again

Teacher Tools

That Will Make Students Love Your Class

James Alan Sturtevant

PUBLICATIONS

Hacking Engagement Again
50 Teacher Tools That Will Make Students Love Your Class

James Sturtevant

Hacking Engagement Again
© 2017 by Times 10 Publications

These books are available at special discounts when purchased in quantity for premiums, promotions, fundraising, and educational use. For inquiries and details, contact us at www.hacklearning.org.

Published by Times 10
Cleveland, OH
HackLearning.org

Project Management by Rebecca Morris
Cover Design by Tracey Henterly
Interior Design by Steven Plummer
Editing and Proofreading by Jennifer Jas

Library of Congress Control Number: 2017945362
ISBN: 978-0-9985705-5-6
First Printing: August, 2017

TABLE OF CONTENTS

P. 45 Express enthusiasm

5

INTRODUCTION

IHATE TO CONFESS this, but my ability to read lengthy books has suffered. I was never a fast reader, but I mastered many long books when I was younger. Currently I'm reading Frank Dikötter's *The Tragedy of Liberation: A History of the Chinese Revolution 1945-1957.* It's a four-hundred-page book, which isn't that long. It's a gripping narrative about mid-20th century Chinese history; however, it's taking me weeks to get through it. The issue is simple: I don't find time during the day to read books, so I try to read when I go to bed. I prop my Kindle on my chest and navigate a few pages before I begin to lose consciousness, and then give up when my Kindle collides with my face.

I'm a curious person and I read a lot of words daily, but the things I read are much shorter than *The Tragedy of Liberation.* I digest vast quantities of web articles and I also listen to a bevy of podcasts. I'm absorbing massive amounts of knowledge, but not in the way I once did. This awareness was a primary ingredient in planning for both my engagement books. *Hacking Engagement Again* is just like its predecessor *Hacking Engagement:* Both are short, containing a little over thirty thousand words apiece. Both are comprised of fifty hacks that are each about six hundred words in length. Neither is intended for linear reading. Instead they're like cookbooks; you scan the table of contents and find what you need to make tomorrow's lesson delicious.

When I wrote *Hacking Engagement,* I was amazed that fifty hacks flowed out of my fingertips and compressed the keys of my laptop. Fifty seemed like a marathon; however, the hacks systematically materialized. When I typed the last period of the last sentence, I thought, *Wow, that was a lot of hacks. I need a break.* What happened next was fascinating.

My neighbor recently bought a scarlet Toyota Prius. I'm not a car guy, but when she pulled up beside me as I walked my dog, I could barely hear her engine, which I thought was cool. It looked sleek and futuristic. Then I asked her about the gas mileage, and this non-car guy instantly became a convert. Later that day, my wife and I went out shopping. Everywhere we drove I saw red Toyota Prii (I was so determined to use this example that I visited Toyota's website and found the official way to refer to Prius plural). The same thing happened when I wrapped up *Hacking Engagement* last summer. I thought I was done writing about engagement tips and tools, but potential hacks kept appearing on my radar: articles I read, colleagues I spoke to, guests I interviewed on my podcast, and most important – lesson plans hatched in my creative incubator of a commute every morning to school. All of these compelled me to write fifty more. My publisher was thrilled.

My favorite book, *The Hitchhiker's Guide to the Galaxy* by Douglas Adams, was published my freshman year of college. It was like reading Monty Python in space. I had lots of assignments for my classes, but I frequently blew those off to read *The Guide.* I loved how the book was like a virtual doorway to deeper understanding. Arthur Dent, the main character, would read about an interesting concept in *The Guide,* press a link, and then learn more virtually. I remember thinking, *Wouldn't it be cool to read a book like that one day?* I did the young me one better; I wrote two books like that! When he wrote his masterpiece in the late 1970s, Douglas Adams predicted that future books would not be confined to their physical front and back covers, but instead be like launching pads to enlightenment. I love how both my engagement books are like such launching pads.

Identical to its older brother, *Hacking Engagement Again* will act as your comprehensive roadmap to create an engaging class that even your reluctant learners will love. Each of the fifty hacks follows an identical template. All begin with a thorough explanation of the problem, then a detailed solution, and finally concrete steps to manifest the solution tomorrow. Despite its ease of consumption, *Hacking Engagement Again* is a powerful and comprehensive tool, but it's also a launching pad.

There are fifty-five QR codes embedded in the hacks. These codes will take you to links where you can learn more, or episodes of the *Hacking Engagement Podcast* where you can hear the fascinating individuals highlighted in the book elaborate on their ideas in compelling conversations with your humble narrator. Before you can take advantage of QR codes, you must have a QR code reader on your mobile device. If you don't have one, I suggest downloading the i-nigma app. It provides a wonderful QR reader and if you navigate to the i-nigma site, you can easily create QR codes too. All the codes in this book were manufactured in this way. Get your feet wet with the intro QR code.

Scan this intro QR code to meet the author.

Just like Arthur Dent learned about the Vogons by pressing a button in *The Hitchhiker's Guide to the Galaxy,* you can learn about HyperDocs and Philosophical Chairs by opening and then walking through the QR code virtual doorways embedded in the hacks. And that's just two examples. There are hacks which will give you creative lesson plan ideas for tomorrow when you need to shake things up. There are hacks that feature tech tools that will enrich your class, be fun to use, and inspire you to use on a regular basis. And there are also templates that will inspire you to fundamentally alter and evolve the way you engage kids.

As I say after the introduction of every episode on my podcast: *Buckle up!* You're going to love *Hacking Engagement Again.*

HACK

CONTEXTUALIZE...
CONTEXTUALIZE...
CONTEXTUALIZE

THE PROBLEM: CHRONOLOGICAL IGNORANCE
IS THE ENEMY OF ENGAGEMENT

I TEACH HISTORY. EVEN as a boy, I was a history nerd. Recently, I was enjoying the company of friends at a party. My buddies all have college degrees and are successful in their chosen professions. A historical topic surfaced. I decided to conduct a little wine-inspired experiment. I just listened to them pontificate about a subject I knew a lot about. This is generally not my disposition when vino veritas is factored in. What took place was fascinating. While my friends had a working understanding of the topic, their background chronology was out of whack, which, of course, did a serious number on their understanding.

If intelligent adults struggle with context on what would seem common historical knowledge, it would be foolhardy to assume that K-12 students, aside from the budding history nerds, would have a clue about the order of events. Contextual ignorance does not just apply to events, but also processes. Students in math, science, and language arts must understand many processes like the quadratic equation, the scientific method, and MLA citation. Chronological awareness with such concepts breeds confidence, which is crucial to engagement. Let's inspire some of that awareness with a cool virtual timeline builder.

THE HACK: CHALLENGE KIDS TO
BUILD A VIRTUAL CHRONOLOGY

ReadWriteThink is a neat website populated by helpful education tools. For this hack, we'll use their online timeline creator. Please follow the QR code in Image 51.1 to access this virtual tool.

Image 51.1

When one thinks of timelines, one typically thinks of historical chronologies. However, the same ordering could be applied to the six steps of the scientific method. The building of this virtual timeline could be a foundational experience for students. Being able to contextualize the steps in a process, or the order of events, fosters academic confidence and opens the door to engagement.

Last semester, my World Civ class was embarking on a unit addressing 20th century Chinese history. My kids knew virtually nothing about this important topic. I decided the first step in this academic journey would be for my kids to create virtual timelines. Here's the prompt I gave students, which can easily be altered to match concepts or processes in other subjects:

- I gave them a starting point (the Boxer Rebellion 1899) and an ending point (the Communist Victory 1949).

- I challenged them to plot seven important events in between.

- I required that each event include a title, the year it took place, an explanation as to why the event was important, and a public domain or creative commons image. (Imagine some of the cool imagery students could find for quadratic equations and the scientific method!)

Once your students complete their timelines, direct them to select the finish button. This is a crucial step on ReadWriteThink. If kids don't hit finish, they may lose what they've created. Once they select finish, they can download a PDF and share it with their classmates and you. See examples in Images 51.2 and 51.3.

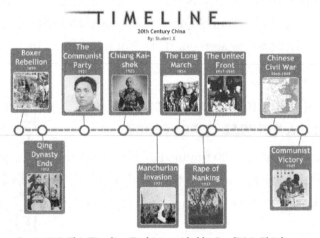

Image 51.2: This Timeline Tool is provided by ReadWriteThink.org, a website developed by the National Council of Teachers of English.

TIMELINE

20th Century China
By: Student X

Items:

○ Boxer Rebellion
This was a chaotic time period when some in China attempted to expell foreign influence. This episode ultimately highlighted the weakness of the Qing Dynasty, and signaled its upcoming demise.

○ Qing Dynasty Ends
The fall of the Qing Dynasty ended absolute monarchy in China. This event elevated the Kuomintang which became the ruling party.

○ The Communist Party
This event inspires a rivalry between the Kuomintang and Communist that will not be resolved till 1949.

○ Chiang Kai-shek
Chiang creates a policy of at times cooperating with, but ultimately destroying the Communist.

○ Manchurian Invasion
This event signifies the opening of hostilities between Japan and China in WWII.

○ The Long March
The decimated Communist retreat to interior. Although a defeat, Mao would morph this event into a powerful Communist legend.

○ Rape of Nanking
This event represents a full scale Japanese invasion of China. It also demonstrates Japan's brutality and determination to intimidate.

○ The United Front
The alliance between the Communist and Nationalists demonstrates the concept of the Enemy of my Enemy is my Friend.

○ Chinese Civil War
This conflict determined which camp would rule China to the present. It also represented an early Cold War proxy conflict.

○ Communist Victory
The Communist victory was not just a triumph for Mao, but for Communism as a world-wide phenomenon. The Communist Chinese victory meant that 25% of the world's population just became Communist.

Image 51.3: This Timeline Tool is provided by ReadWriteThink.org, a website developed by the National Council of Teachers of English.

The next day, the teacher can formulate small groups so students can compare timelines. There'll be lively discussion about event choices, image choices, and explaining to one another why they found certain events, or junctures in a process, important.

Kids are honest. Instructors can learn a lot from unsolicited feedback. Many students commented about how much the creation of this timeline helped them prepare for the topic. Prompting students to contextualize is powerful.

WHAT YOU CAN DO TOMORROW

- **Create your own timeline on ReadWriteThink.** This will familiarize you with the process. Select finish, and download the image as a PDF.

- **Select an important topic.** This would be a great introduction for a unit. It could also be used effectively for describing the steps in a process.

- **Formulate small discussion groups.** After the timelines are created, students should compare and contrast their timelines with classmates. This will further help kids contextualize because peers may have included events they didn't consider.

When students are able to place events or processes in context, they become confident and engaged academic explorers.

RECRUIT STUDENTS TO EMBARK ON AN ACADEMIC HERO'S JOURNEY

THE PROBLEM: STUDENTS RARELY CELEBRATE, MUCH LESS ACKNOWLEDGE, THEIR ACADEMIC ACCOMPLISHMENTS

IT WAS MY first day as a third-grade student. Our teacher was calling each of us to her desk to turn in the reams of paperwork that schools used to require on day one. As I waited my turn, I leafed through my new textbook, pausing on the pictures. I navigated toward the end of the book, and the final math section startled me. The pages were populated with very advanced-looking equations. They seemed like the scribblings of a mad scientist on his chalkboard. I wondered, *Wow. That looks complicated. I don't know if I'll be able to do these problems.* Nine months later, school was about to dismiss for summer. Remarkably, we were breezing through the unit with the equations that looked so intimidating. I vividly remember thinking, *I thought these problems were going to be hard, but they're easy. I need to remember this next year.* I give the young me a lot of credit for this mental vote of confidence.

THE HACK: INSPIRE FUTURE CONFIDENCE BY CHALLENGING STUDENTS TO CHRONICLE A PAST ACHIEVEMENT

Lisa Highfill, Kelly Hilton, and Sarah Landis are the co-creators of HyperDocs. These ladies have designed a remarkable website that provides teachers with digital lesson templates and plenty of sample HyperDocs. Aside from their outstanding organization, the templates are beautiful, which should never be underestimated. To begin creating, simply FILE>MAKE A COPY and complete the stages of the lesson cycle by adding instructions and resources. The HyperDoc Girls have a template for the Hero's Journey. Their template contains five stages:

Phase 1: The Call to Adventure
Phase 2: Entering the Unknown
Phase 3: Meeting the Mentor
Phase 4: Transformation
Phase 5: Mastery

Follow the QR code in Image 52.1 to access the HyperDoc Girls website, and scroll down to reach the Hero's Journey template. This hack will inspire students to recreate an academic hero's journey.

Conduct a brainstorming session. This can be done individually, or in small groups. Prompt kids to list their proudest academic achievements. Under each achievement, students should then record obstacles they had to overcome. Once completed, students need to designate the one challenge they found particularly thorny. This will become their hero's quest.

Image 52.1

Provide students with a link to the Hero's Journey HyperDoc template. Instruct them to make a copy. Challenge kids to research the hero's journey stages. What does each mean? What would make good examples for each stage? The HyperDoc template should act like a storyboard. Students can insert images, text, and links. Once completed, they can then take their storyboard and produce something awesome. They could record a podcast, craft a mural, perform a skit, or create a video.

The final stage of the academic hero's quest will be to create a narrative. This exercise asks students to take what they've learned through recounting a past success and then apply it to the present. Prompt students to formulate a plan on how they can replicate success when complicated challenges arise in your class this semester. Access Image 52.2 to hear my conversation with the HyperDoc Girls.

Image 52.2

WHAT YOU CAN DO TOMORROW

- **Recount a personal story of academic success.** Often, students are convinced their teachers just breezed through school. Tell your students about an academic obstacle you found particularly challenging, and explain how you ultimately prevailed! This will help humanize you and perhaps inspire your kids.

- **Inspire students to designate a personal success for the academic hero's quest.** If students are totally stumped, you may even let them use a non-academic example.

- **Expose kids to the HyperDoc Girls Hero's Journey template.** This wonderful template will be the journey storyboard. They will create their productions from this lesson flow.

- **Guide students toward applying this success to the current semester.** I suggested a narrative, but it could be another format. The key is for kids to internalize this: *I succeeded before. I can do it again.*

By reliving a past success, students will be more willing to embark on another academic hero's quest.

 **HACK**

 **TUNE IN THE 21ST CENTURY WALKIE-TALKIE**

THE PROBLEM: BOYS AREN'T EXCITED ABOUT READING

W HEN I WAS in third grade, the last thing in the world I wanted to do was read a book. What was true then is still true today for many young boys.

Debbie Olsen, an inclusion teacher from Long Island, New York, certainly recognizes this attitude. So she decided to use Voxer, the 21st century walkie talkie app, to get nine-year-old boys excited about reading. She says, "I began using Voxer for a book club. I would like to tell you that I put a lot of thought and careful planning into this, but that would not be true. My gut instinct was that Voxer could be a "hook" to motivate these readers, so I ran with it."

I was instantly drawn to Debbie's idea! My first reaction when I started playing with Voxer was, *This is a lot like the walkie-talkie set I got on my tenth birthday.* I loved that toy! My posse and I played with them constantly in my little neighborhood. There were only two units that we had to share, and from a performance standpoint, my ancient walkie-talkie sucked! That's not the case with Voxer. Its range is global and its sound quality is solid. The major

Students will be excited about using this tool and the reading will be the vehicle.

issue is inadvertent butt-voxing from a phone in a back pocket. I once transmitted a fifteen-minute dead air vox to my teacher group. Fortunately, I didn't say or do anything too stupid during that marathon!

THE HACK: CREATE A VOXER BOOK CLUB

Here's how Debbie created her Voxer book club: "I sent a letter home to their parents asking them to download the free Voxer app. I told the boys about a special project we were going to try."

She continues, "I then demonstrated how Voxer works. I had asked a colleague from another school to be ready to vox with me. My class watched in amazement as I chatted back and forth with my remote friend. We even used some CB lingo, *Breaker, breaker. What's your 20?* The boys literally went nuts! The goal was to make it fun and get them voxing first before I tried to get them voxing about the book. The first night, the boys voxed a million times. I listened but did not respond. There were some ridiculous voxes with sounds and general boy silliness. The next day, we discussed how fun it was to use Voxer, but also about being respectful."

First, Debbie got her kids hooked on Voxer, and then she hooked them on the book. "I then gave out the books and told the boys it was theirs to keep. They loved that! We planned how much reading they thought they would be able to do for the

Image 53.1

day (both in and out of school). I did not say that they had to vox each day. I let that happen naturally. Every one of them had multiple voxes each evening." Follow Image 53.1 to hear Debbie discuss her Voxer-infused lesson plan.

Boy, I wish I could have experienced Debbie's class as a third-grader!

WHAT YOU CAN DO TOMORROW

- **Craft a letter to parents explaining your objectives.** Some parents may object to their child participating in Voxer or downloading the app. Have these students form a separate book club and they can meet and discuss in person.

- **Demonstrate Voxer.** This was a brilliant idea on Debbie's part! A successful demonstration is a great hook.

- **Designate a reading for the full Voxer book club treatment.** Voxer is your hook! Students will be excited about using this tool and the reading will be the vehicle. Choose a reading that will elicit great discussion.

Create a Voxer book club. It's a cool way to hook reluctant readers.

HACK

LAY DOWN THE 15-WORD GAUNTLET

THE PROBLEM: STUDENT PRESENTATION DAY IS BORING

I ONCE GOT TOO windy in my college speech class. I looked out from the lectern at a stunned and disengaged audience. They seemed to be rapidly losing their meager remaining focus. I did what presenters in such situations often do, I talked more. After class, my professor pulled me aside and in a motherly way, uttered words from Shakespeare that changed my life, "Young Mr. Sturtevant, brevity is the soul of wit." Her words were transformational.

The fifteen-word limit encourages creativity.

This story is applicable to engagement, because I've suffered through painfully boring student presentations. And if I was bored, think of the other students. Let's strive to make such presentations:

- More attractive

- More engaging

- Less time-consuming

- More interactive

In order to create such presentations, we must first run the gauntlet.

THE HACK: LAY DOWN THE FIFTEEN-WORD GAUNTLET

According to various sources, fifteen to twenty words is the average sentence length. That seemed long, till I actually wrote a sentence:

> When I was in high school, I would have laughed uproariously if anyone had informed me that I was destined to be a teacher. (24 words)

Challenge students to embrace Shakespeare's quote about brevity. Limit their text on presentation slides to fifteen words. This will be a wonderful challenge for your students. They may revolt. Not only is it important to reduce the number of words, the limit will also hopefully dissuade copying and pasting. This awful practice flirts with plagiarism and makes for exceedingly dull presentations as students drone the words of another.

The fifteen-word limit encourages creativity. Students must populate slides with attractive images. They must animate slides with captivating stories. This leads to far more engaging presentations. Another option is to challenge students to limit the text on each slide to one hundred and forty characters, like a tweet. But let them know they still need to spell correctly: U cannot replace you.

WHAT YOU CAN DO TOMORROW

- **Direct students to create a one-sentence description of themselves.** This is a hilarious activity. After a few minutes, have kids count words in their one-sentence descriptive masterpieces.

- **Create the *fifteen-word Berlin Wall* or the *fifteen-word 38th Parallel*.** Attach a long piece of masking tape to your floor, dividing the room in half. Direct students whose descriptive sentences are longer than fifteen words to stand on one side of the tape, and those with less than fifteen to stand on the other side. Those who have exactly fifteen words can straddle the tape.

- **Display fifteen-word examples on the board.** Praise students who hit the fifteen-word mark, and write their sentences on the board. Tell students that this is the perfect sentence length. If you don't have any students who wrote exactly fifteen words, choose a student who was close.

- **Display the longest and shortest sentences.** Direct the student who created the longest sentence and the student who created the shortest to write their sentences on the board too. Discuss how adjusting the length of these examples could improve them.
- **Inform students about the fifteen-word maximum for the next presentation.** Discuss the positives and negatives to this directive. Also, discuss obstacles to its implementation.

Student presentations tend to be boring. Let's make them engaging instead. Foster student creativity by limiting kids to fifteen words per slide.

HACK

CLIMB ABOARD TRACY'S TRAIN

THE PROBLEM: SOME TALENTED STUDENTS AREN'T MOTIVATED TO DO ENRICHMENT WORK

Y WIFE AND I are public educators, so you can probably guess our salary range, but we consider ourselves immensely rich. I'm darned content with my life. Occasionally, however, wealthier friends and relatives will expose us to life's finer things. Guess what? Many of those luxuries are pretty awesome. I once slurped an expensive California Cab, and *Damn!* My very successful brother-in-law got me floor seats to a Cleveland Cavaliers game. And recently, a wealthy friend rented a stretch limo and took a group of us out on the town. These were really cool experiences I'd love to repeat.

What would happen if you turned enrichment into a stretch limo or NBA floor seats? Tracy Enos did just that. She's an eighth-grade ELA teacher from West Warwick, Rhode Island. Tracy strove to make enrichment cool, desirable, and exclusive. She succeeded. In her class, kids want to extend and explore. The way they gain access to this enriched content is to board *The Train*. See Image 55.1 for Tracy's intro page.

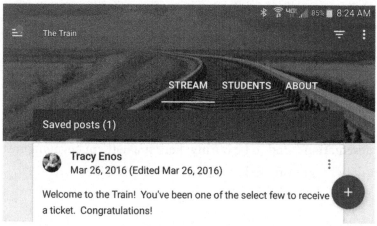

Image 55.1: Google and the Google logo are registered trademarks of Google Inc., used with permission.

THE HACK: CREATE AN EXCLUSIVE VIRTUAL CLASSROOM INSIDE YOUR TRADITIONAL CLASSROOM

Tracy created *The Train* as a separate Google Classroom just for enrichment. This wonderful name begs all sorts of metaphors:

- All aboard
- The train is leaving the station; don't be left behind
- The train is picking up speed
- This train is going places
- She's comin' round the bend. Are you going to hop on?

Catchy statements such as this are ultra engaging. I wouldn't want to be left off the train. Here's how Tracy describes her students' fascination with the train: "A student asked me if they were on the train. I told them not yet, but you could be! I sent invite codes to 16 students. What I found is students who didn't get an invite code were determined to get one. That's exactly what I wanted to happen."

Tracy doesn't view traveling on the train as a one-semester journey. "Once you're on the train, you can remain on the train. That even applies to kids who move to the high school. I want them to collaborate next year with new passengers!"

Finally, there's a warning label attached to this hack. When you're successful at building this yearning for enrichment, you may end up with some snarky and entitled train passengers. Be prepared to manage this, but recognize it for what it is – a sign of success. Open Image 55.2 to hear some of my students describe their affection for this idea.

Image 55.2

WHAT YOU CAN DO TOMORROW

- **Create a list of students you'd like to extend.** It could be based on grades, work ethic, creativity, or an ability to express. I like to make enrichment widely available. If a kid wants to give it a try, I say, *Go for it.*

- **Create a separate Google Classroom for enrichment.** This will be your hub of activity that students with invite codes can access.

- **Create a cool name for your semi-secret society.** *The Train* is truly epic because it can be morphed so easily.

- **Manage passenger snobbery.** Some enrichment kids might put on airs. If this happens, please manage it. However, take solace in the fact that it is a wonderful sign of success.

Talented students who aren't challenged are sometimes hard to motivate. Create an enticing virtual classroom inside your traditional classroom.

HACK

EXPOSE STUDENT PHONE OBSESSION

THE PROBLEM: TEENS ARE DISTRACTED BY THEIR PHONES

PICTURE THIS. YOU'RE pontificating to students and you're bringing it! You're like Moses on Mount Sinai. You're certain you'll soon be invited to the governor's mansion to receive your *Teacher of the Year Award*. But just before you launch into your epic closing argument, you're swept by a wave of devastation. You notice that a significant number of your students are missing this grand learning opportunity because they're staring intensely at their laps. Unfortunately, you know why. They're checking a new batch of notifications, or maybe putting that sweet pair of shoes on their Amazon wish list, and trying to finish before you notice them obsessing over their screens.

I'm more comfortable with enlightenment over prohibition.

As a contemporary instructor, I've felt this profound burn, and I bet you have too. Some teachers are totally hard-nosed. They don't give the kids an inch on phone use during instruction. If that's you, respect. However, I, like many teachers, am not so stern when it comes to students and their phones. Plus, kids are darned adept at subtle screen time. And let's not forget, students can use their devices in class in the pursuit of knowledge. While I'm uncomfortable with prohibition, I'd certainly love to see kids stare at their phones less during strategic moments of instruction.

THE HACK: PROMOTE OVERUSE MINDFULNESS

I recently became more cognizant of my own phone overuse. This awareness was birthed thanks to a cool little app called Moment. Follow the QR code in Image 56.1 to access the web page.

I'm more comfortable with enlightenment over prohibition. I'm more comfortable giving students tools and information, having them apply it to their existence, and then hoping it makes an impact. The Moment app tracks daily screen time. Of course, I applied it to myself first. I've read various stats pertaining to average daily phone use. Most data pegs usage at around four hours! That seemed exorbitant till I started measuring my usage. I was horrified.

Image 56.1

Challenge your kids to do what I did. Have them download the Moment app (currently only available for Apple products; but QualityTime is a similar app for Android) and measure their phone usage for one week. It would be even more engaging if you could tie the experience to an idea you're studying. Such a week-long experiment is perfect for learning about mindfulness, attention span, time management, sedentary lifestyles, interpersonal skills, and attachment. Regardless of the link to your curriculum, it's important that students reflect upon their experience. I challenged my students to create a blog post about their new awareness of screen time, but that is just one option. It's also important for kids to apply the experience. Prompt your students to report how this new information will influence future behavior. Hopefully, their response won't be, "It won't." Please don't take it personally if

Image 56.2

you get this reply. You nonetheless planted a seed. It may take a while to grow. Aim your QR code reader at Image 56.2 to hear Nahom, one of my kids, discuss his week using Moment.

WHAT YOU CAN DO TOMORROW

- **Download the app and track your screen time.** This might be ultra humbling. I was shocked. Such an experience might help you avoid charges of hypocrisy when you get on your phone-abuse high horse.

- **Create a prompt based on your curriculum.** This challenge will be engaging, but scheme how you can incorporate it into your curriculum.

- **Challenge students to track their phone use for one week.** I was amazed at some of the unsolicited conversations that surfaced in class when students ambled in each morning. One young lady informed me, "I went over eight hours yesterday."

Perhaps a great way to manage phone addiction is simple awareness. While it might not convert all your students, I'll wager that many of your students, like Nahom, will become determined to make changes.

═ HACK ═

TASTE THE ENGAGEMENT

THE PROBLEM: FOOD IS NOT LIVING UP TO ITS ACADEMIC ENGAGEMENT POTENTIAL

OUR DRIVE TO consume food is paramount. Sure, your commitment to protecting loved ones, or perhaps your basic will to live, might be on top – at least that's what your full belly thinks. Teenage boys snigger about their sex drive being strongest. But those who are inclined to demote hunger and elevate their courageous natures, or their hormones, probably have never been really hungry. I doubt I have, but I have zero problems embracing the powerful force of food as a driver of life itself. So I say, *Why not harness this epic force of nature to engage students?*

I recently had a popular student teacher say *bon voyage* to my class. We decided to throw him a Napoleon Dynamite Cookie Party. Each student brought a sweet treat for themselves and two friends. A few good citizens volunteered to bake batches of cookies to feed the multitudes. On party day, we munched, yakked, hugged, offered farewells, laughed at each other's sugar highs, and watched a ridiculous movie most students had seen ten times.

My student teacher's going away party reflects how food has usually been offered in classrooms. It's a treat. It's celebratory. It's a way to break the routine. But that's the old paradigm; let's get serious about harnessing the amazing engaging potential of food.

THE HACK: USE FOOD TO TEACH AN ENGAGING LESSON

I teach a unit on Buddhism in my World Civ class. Mindfulness is a foundation of the Eightfold Path. It's tough for spastic 21st century teens to grasp mindfulness. However, they constantly think and talk about food. Prompting students to blog about eating a conscious meal is the way to capitalize on this obsession. Follow Image 57.1 to read my consumption prompt.

Follow the QR code in Image 57.2 to hear one of my students describe how her understanding deepened as she prepared a meal for her family.

Image 57.1

I teach history, but other subjects can use food obsession too. Have students:

- Create pies for Pi Day in math.

- Create a high-fiber snack for biology or health.

- Create a dessert that matches a foreign language class.

- Create a vegan snack for their demonstration speech in language arts.

- Create a full Greek symposium simulation in philosophy (substitute grape juice for wine).

Image 57.2

It's not enough, however, for food to be a prop, or to merely add to the ambiance. Food can act as a vehicle to inspire deeper thought:

- Why are circles important?

- Why are pies shaped like circles?

- Why is consuming fiber important?

- Why do cultures have different cuisines?

- Why has veganism emerged?

- Why was the symposium symbolic of ancient Greek culture?

WHAT YOU CAN DO TOMORROW

- **Create a food prompt that teaches.** Brainstorm food options with your students.

- **Challenge students to chronicle the preparation and consumption process.** Have students record how they made it and ate it. This could be a blog, a journal entry, a YouTube video, a podcast, or a photo slideshow.

- **Inspire students to make broader applications.** Prompt students to go deeper. Review my follow-up questions for ideas.

Food consumption is a powerful driving force. Use this passion to engage students.

HACK

NAVIGATE THE ROLLING SEAS OF CONTROVERSIAL TOPICS

THE PROBLEM: TEACHERS AREN'T CERTAIN HOW TO ADDRESS CONTROVERSIAL TOPICS

I'VE TAUGHT FOR more than three decades. Thousands of students have claimed Mr. Sturtevant. Those multitudes have learned about religions. I teach in a conservative community, and unfortunately, some adults worry about exposing kids to various faiths. That's too bad. Only one third of the world is Christian. It's good for students to learn about the diverse faith traditions of the majority of the planet's inhabitants. Exposure to different cultures is not a threat. I've yet to have a student inform me, "Mr. Sturtevant, because you taught me about the Five Pillars, I no longer want to be a Christian. I'm now converting to Islam."

Unfortunately, teaching about religion is controversial, but controversial topics are by their very nature engaging. In the case of religion, teach don't preach. As long as you're on the "*This faith believes this*" track, and stay off the "*This is what you should believe*" path, you should be fine. I have no interest in converting my students. My kids aren't sure of my faith affiliation. That's the way I like it and my students seem to prefer it.

The objective is a conversation instead of confrontation.

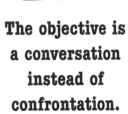

THE HACK: TEACH A CONTROVERSIAL TOPIC OBJECTIVELY

Before you set off on your controversial topics voyage, have a conversation with your principal. Tell her, "These are some potentially controversial topics we might discuss this semester. This is how I plan to include this subject in a unit. Is there anything we need to discuss?" Your principal will hopefully be grateful for this heads-up. Perhaps your principal will have fantastic suggestions on how to engage students. Or you might hear, "Sorry, teaching about the Five Pillars is off limits at this school." Such an administrative preemptive strike at least lets you know exactly where you stand. You'll then have to make a professional decision on how to proceed.

Image 58.1

My passionate advice is to approach controversial topics in an agendaless fashion. If you're out to prove that global warming is a conspiracy by secular socialist scientists, it will turn off every student who disagrees with you. Once partisan flags are unfurled, people stop listening and start broadcasting, often obnoxiously. Turn your students into investigators instead of advocates. That's why Socratic seminars are so powerful. The objective is a conversation instead of confrontation.

My favorite tactic for controversial topics is to morph student perspective. A wonderful tool is to expose students to the *Belief-O-Matic* online survey. Access the *Belief-O-Matic* page in Image 58.1.

The site includes twenty questions that measure disposition and aims to help people find the faith that matches their beliefs. Once students submit their guesses,

Belief-O-Matic emails results in the form of percentage affiliation. Here's a neat little twist: Challenge students to answer the questions as a Muslim or a Confucist. In other words, break them out of their limited perspective. You can use it as an assessment tool! While they're taking the survey, student engagement skyrockets! It's tough to answer as someone else. It's also cool how everyone giggles and relaxes. Kids often complete the survey again answering authentically. Teaching

Image 58.2

controversial topics doesn't have to inspire open warfare. Follow Image 58.2 to hear my thoughts on how teachers should handle controversial elections.

WHAT YOU CAN DO TOMORROW

- **Create a list of potentially controversial course topics.** Some topics, like abortion, are probably too risky.
- **Consult with your principal.** Give her a heads-up as to your plans. She may have great ideas for your lesson; or she could slam on the brakes. Regardless, it's better to have the conversation in the planning phases.
- **Teach about…don't indoctrinate.** The goal is to help students explore.

Controversial topics are engaging. Get prior approval, and then present them in an objective fashion.

HACK

REBEL AGAINST
THE BELL

THE PROBLEM: THE FIFTY-MINUTE CLASS PERIOD IS LIMITING

KIDS ARE JUST starting to get it. They're finally opening up in a discussion, they're finding great resources for a research paper, they're starting to harmonize in choir, their sculptures are just beginning to take shape, their findings in a science experiment are just about to materialize – and then the bell rings.

This frequently happens to Melissa Maxson's devoted art students. You know you've engaged kids when they say, "Dang, I can't believe the period is over." Melissa hears this daily. She became frustrated with the industrial-assembly-line nature of the school day with its uniform fifty-minute modules. So, she detonated space/time limitations. Now, her classroom is the world and no bells disrupt creative trances.

THE HACK: CREATE AN EXTRACURRICULAR CLUB FOR YOUR CLASS

Melissa described her predicament and her solution: "In art class, it takes time to set up and clean up. This drastically limits student creativity. Often, they'll just be getting into it and it will be time to wrap up. In my after-school art club, kids can create without time restrictions."

But Melissa's club isn't just for students who want extra project time, it's also a community. Students bond, discuss art, watch videos, or just hang out. Service is one of the primary goals of this little after-school artist colony. Melissa's club considers their school building a blank needy canvas in desperate need of a little teen artistic swag. They've painted murals in the hallways outside of classrooms. The images were inspired by the subjects taught on the other sides of the walls. They made going to the restroom fascinating by adorning the walls with intriguing intricate collages. Her school's bathrooms are the most inspirational in the history of public education.

Her artist colony's last beautification project was truly epic. Her students painted the ceiling tiles in the school's main hallway (see Image 59.1). Not only were her artists engaged in this home improvement project, but so were their classmates. It was hilarious to watch the chain reaction installation day. One student would look up and point and then others would follow suit. There was a whole lot of bumping into each other as they stared up and gawked. Please consider destroying the space/time nature of your class.

Image 59.1

WHAT YOU CAN DO TOMORROW

- **Create an extracurricular club for your class.** Take engaged students from your traditional class time period and create an after-school vanguard filled with rich expression, deep exploration, and profound engagement.
- **Investigate a project opportunity.** Similar to Melissa's art club, engage your club members with a school or community project.
- **List ways to promote your club, your class club, and your club's project.** A successful after-school club could make you and your class kid magnets.

Don't be limited by the traditional fifty-minute class period. Create an after-school club based on your class.

HACK

ENGAGE IN COMPETITION AND THEN ENGAGE ABOUT COMPETITION

THE PROBLEM: YOUR CLASS NEEDS AN ENERGY INFUSION

CLICHÉS ARE OFTEN accepted as truth. No one questions their veracity. This is odd. My entire life, I've heard this cliché about competition blathered enthusiastically: *Competition brings out the best in us.* To a large degree, I embrace it. Competition in the classroom can infuse a serious adrenaline rush, but there are trade-offs. People can get carried away when competition is involved. Have you ever witnessed adult behavior at youth sporting events?

My ninth-grade Global Studies class recently competed in two contests designed to apply concepts from the Industrial Revolution. Students didn't anticipate, however, that the simulations would spawn an intense discourse on human nature and challenge the vague cliché about competition.

THE HACK: USE CLASSROOM COMPETITION
AS A VEHICLE FOR ENGAGEMENT

On the first day of the simulation, students became artisans. They were tasked to draw a person from head to toe. Some kids were terrible drawers. No one cared. Some of the awful drawings were celebrated when students shared their master-

Competition provides a classroom with an adrenaline rush.

pieces. We voted which ones we liked best, and those talented artists were rewarded with a Reese's Cup. Good times were had by all.

On day two, students mass-produced the superior drawings. Even the celebrated artists from the previous day were inserted unceremoniously onto the assembly line. I divided the class into competing teams. Each student was assigned a body part to reproduce. Sheets of paper moved along the assembly line (a row of desks) and images far inferior to the originals emerged. In the spirit of unbridled capitalism, I promised that the team that produced the most quality pictures would be rewarded with restroom passes. I warned students that I didn't have enough passes for everyone on each team. I bellowed, "Slackers will not be rewarded!" This created instant intra-team animosity.

After ten minutes, I mercifully ended the production day. The knives came out immediately! Students on the successful team quickly ratted out slackers and made it clear they should receive no reward. It was epic.

I challenged students to respond to the following debriefing on a Google Form:

- How did the simulation compare to the Industrial Revolution?

- What was the difference between being an artisan and an unskilled laborer?

- What were the pros and cons to the different methods of production?

Student engagement was strong throughout this simulation, but it peaked with the final prompt:

Come up with a new cliché about competition.

This prompt could be used in any class or any subject that incorporates competition. I had my students post their responses on a Padlet virtual bulletin board. Many included images, links, and videos with their posts.

WHAT YOU CAN DO TOMORROW

- **Have your students compete in a game or simulation.** If you can't create one, you can probably find a competition online for almost any unit in any subject.

- **Stress your students out!** You want to ensure elevated tension and elevated stakes.

- **Conduct a formative assessment.** Create a few reflective prompts to distribute after the competition. The prompts could inspire a class discussion, but I love the 100% participation nature of Google Forms.

- **Have students post their new clichés.** This is the engaging take-home! Padlet is a great option, but if the internet is not an option, use a poster and sticky notes.

Competition provides a classroom with an adrenaline rush. Use this experience to engage students about larger topics.

ACK

STAGE STUDENT PRESENTATIONS IN MINUTES

THE PROBLEM: MANY STUDENT PRESENTATIONS ARE NOT ENGAGING

A FEW YEARS AGO, my students endured two days of student presentations. A few kids put a lot of prep time in and were passionate about presenting. Unfortunately, they were a distinct minority. Most of the presentations were as dry as an August lawn! The drab performances were low-energy, filled with endless bullet points, and were rehashing tired topics. Once a student gave a presentation or grasped a concept, he had little incentive to listen to the next gabfest from a classmate. I vowed that I wasn't going to do this to my kids again!

THE HACK: THE GALLERY WALK

To enhance engagement when it comes to student presentations, please try the Gallery Walk. It's a simple but profound tactic. The instructor must first settle on the number of topics to be covered. I like designating three big essential concepts because three translates to tidy student groups of three. It's best to keep topics at a lower number so the presentation groups don't get too big. The teacher then randomly assigns students a number from one to three:

- Students with number 1 will demonstrate Topic A.

- Students with number 2 will demonstrate Topic B.

- Students with number 3 will demonstrate Topic C.

At this juncture, teachers are faced with a choice. They can have all the students assigned the number 1 work together on a project about Topic A, or each student can produce independently. After students complete their projects, the gallery is ready to be constructed!

The Gallery Walk functions like this:

- Each table is an exhibit. Students place their completed projects on the table that coincides with their number.

- Students play the roles of curator (presenter) and visitor. Kids will present once and listen twice.

- Each exhibit stop will be timed. I like three minutes. It's been my experience that such a time limit fosters productivity. The curator presents for two minutes and then visitors ask questions and record reflections for the remaining minute.

- At the conclusion of the three-exhibit circuit, the entire class convenes for debriefing.

Gallery A

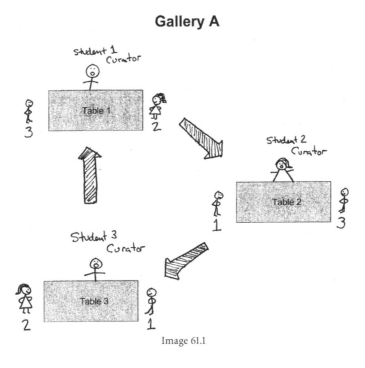

Image 61.1

I showed the sketch in Image 61.1 to my students to demonstrate the process.

The biggest challenge with the Gallery Walk is student number logistics. I had a class of twenty-seven last semester, which was perfect. I created three galleries each with nine students. I set it up in the following fashion:

Gallery A:	Gallery B:	Gallery C:
Table 1	Table 1	Table 1
Table 2	Table 2	Table 2
Table 3	Table 3	Table 3

But alas, two students were absent on presentation day, which totally detonated my perfect arrangement. No worries. I merely had those kids in short-handed groups temporarily migrate to other exhibits or even galleries when needed. You can also tinker with four groups of four, and five groups of five. But be prepared to do some mixing and matching because rarely do you have a perfect multiple and kids invariably miss on presentation day. You can also take some students who really work well

together and have them circulate through the gallery. Don't let number logistics intimidate you! Open Image 61.2 to access my blog about the Gallery Walk, and you can read my prompts, review my *Visitor's Impressions* sheet, watch a brief instructional video, and listen to a podcast featuring students who rave about this method in comparison to the old-school blab fest.

Image 61.2

WHAT YOU CAN DO TOMORROW

- **Designate three to five concepts that you'd like for students to present.** These should be big ideas from your unit.

- **Randomly group students.** If you have three big topics, number them off in threes.

- **Sort kids into galleries.** Think of each gallery as a presentation circuit. Refer to the diagram or follow the link to my blog if you need more direction.

- **Create a *Visitor's Impressions* handout.** This is where students can record their thoughts, or respond to prompts when they're in listening mode.

Student presentations do not have to be a tedious marathon. Institute the Gallery Walk and watch engagement blossom.

HACK

MULTIPLY YOURSELF BY 26 WITH CLASS PLAYLISTS

THE PROBLEM: THE TRADITIONAL ONE-SIZE-FITS-ALL LESSON UNDERMINES PERSONALIZATION

I LOVE SPOTIFY. I'VE created a number of cool playlists. Not to brag, but my music is known to get guests moving at parties. Most of my playlists consist of songs from my younger days – 1970s and 80s R&B. My wife enjoys much of my music, but not all. When I do chores around the house, I often put on my headphones and listen to some of my more ostentatious old-skool jamz that I'm certain my wife won't like. In other words, I personalize my musical consumption. That's the beauty of playlists. They provide anytime, anywhere tunes on demand. Wouldn't it be cool if we could personalize tomorrow's lesson in the same way?

The tasks inside the playlists represent rungs of a ladder leading to higher levels of thinking.

THE HACK: INTRODUCE CLASS PLAYLISTS TO FACILITATE EPIC PERSONALIZATION

Tracy Enos and her twin sister, Heather Roberti, are two outstanding middle school educators from West

Warwick, Rhode Island. Tracy teaches ELA and Heather is a math teacher. Both enlightened me about the beauty of class playlists – and now we're talking about playlists of educational activities, not songs. The idea is simple, elegant, and contemporary: Teachers craft a menu of playlists that are tailored to various student needs and abilities, and each playlist includes a number of tasks. Teachers can then suggest that kids gravitate toward a playlist best suited to them. The tasks inside the playlists represent rungs of a ladder leading to higher levels of thinking.

Kids get playlists. They use them daily. Playlists put them in control, just like when they insert their earbuds and decide which song to play next. So when you announce tomorrow that you're introducing learning playlists, you'll automatically have a certain level of buy-in thanks to the familiarity of the concept.

Image 62.1

Essential to the creation of magnetic playlists are beautiful templates. And that, dear reader, is where HyperDocs waltzes into this narrative. HyperDocs are souped-up Google Docs that can include links, images, and more. HyperDocs provide templates that make the creation of beautiful and well-organized playlists possible. Lisa Highfill, Kelly Hilton, and Sarah Landis are the HyperDoc Girls. Please follow the QR code in Image 62.1 to visit their website, where you can find tremendous HyperDocs templates that are available to educators for free.

Image 62.2

Tracy and Heather have engineered highly personalized instruction leveraging class playlists created with HyperDocs templates. See an example in Image 62.2.

Heather assesses student learning via Google Forms during each phase of the playlist. She mentioned how introducing playlists to her repertoire was like creating twenty-six versions of herself interacting with kids virtually and then often personally. Tracy said that if a visitor were to enter her room during instruction, she would seem more like a waitress than a teacher…circulating from table to table and joyfully interacting with individuals and groups. Open Image 62.3 to hear Tracy and Heather talk more

Image 62.3

about student playlists.

WHAT YOU CAN DO TOMORROW

- **Make a list of at least three activities for your playlist.** These could be flipped lectures, videos, web quests, writing prompts, research prompts, or any activity germane to your lesson.

- **Adapt your playlist to make a version for advanced students and one for students who may struggle.** You can then steer kids toward the best match.

- **Navigate to the HyperDoc Girls website and choose an attractive template.** This website makes the creation of playlists easy. You'll be amazed at your organized and attractive creation.

- **Tomorrow, to begin class, display one of your iTunes or Spotify playlists on your smartboard and then play some old-people music.** You could even blather about why a song is meaningful. This is a wonderful and cheesy way to introduce the empowering nature of playlists.

There's an old saying that when in Rome, do as the Romans do. So in attempting to engage contemporary young people, use things they like to use, like playlists.

HACK

FENG SHUI YOUR STUDENTS

THE PROBLEM: OUR CURRICULUM SEEMS REMARKABLY REMOVED FROM STUDENTS' EVERYDAY EXISTENCE

I WAS CHILLING IN my classroom two days before Christmas break. As I surveyed my digs, I became disgusted with myself. My room was a mess. I had just been

In the midst of all this personal improvement, students will see the relevant nature of the unit you're studying.

enlightening my students about the awesome Asian concept of Chi…an invisible source of energy that permeates the universe. Chi flows through the environment, animals, and people, as well as man-made structures. Acupuncture and Tai Chi stimulate the life-giving flow of Chi through a person. The ancient interior decoration practice of Feng Shui can do the same for your home or workspace. I felt like a hypocrite. I decided my room was in desperate need of a Feng Shui makeover.

THE HACK: APPLY A CONCEPT FROM YOUR CLASS IN A DEMONSTRABLE WAY

I decided to engage in a little self-improvement and demonstrate a complex topic from class, right in front of my students' eyes. I would then challenge them to do the same. This exercise had great potential:

- I could apply a complex topic from class in a demonstrable way.

- I could become more approachable to my students as they cheered me on in my noble quest.

- I could inspire kids to apply Feng Shui to some aspect of their lives.

- My room would become more livable.

This is EXACTLY what happened! When students returned in January, they were impressed with my orderly flowing room. I issued the Feng Shui Challenge in my maiden January student blog prompt. They could Feng Shui their rooms, or lockers, or cars, or phones. Open the QR code in Image 63.1 to read my blog prompt, "Feng Shui Your Room."

Image 63.1

Please be aware, this doesn't just have to be a social studies thing. You could set a personal goal in nutrition, exercise, time management, interpersonal skills, or to become more charitable. Then, you need to tell your kids about it. Explain what you're trying to accomplish and why. Describe how this evolution will benefit you and why students should join you in your quest. Link your objective to your subject.

In the goals I listed above, it would be easy to create data measures, which could be linked to math and science. Think broadly. Wouldn't it be cool to improve in front of your students and then have them select areas to improve? In the midst of all this personal improvement, students will see the relevant nature of the unit you're studying. The coolest aspect that must be emphasized is that my students understood Feng Shui. They saw me apply the principles, and then they applied

Image 63.2

them to their own lives. These engaging real-life experiences lead to deep understanding. Hear more about the Feng Shui Challenge from my podcast in Image 63.2.

WHAT YOU CAN DO TOMORROW

- **Search your curriculum for a concept you can apply.** Students often question the relevancy of subjects. This is a golden opportunity to master such inquiries.

- **Brainstorm a way to demonstrate your application.** This is the challenging part, but the payoff is huge.

- **Concoct a way to challenge students to do the same.** After you demonstrate your self-improvement, challenge students to follow suit. When students filed into my room after Christmas break, they were impressed with how it flowed. They were then amenable to give Feng Shui a try. Some kids were quite motivated.

- **Have them share their experiences in a demonstrable way.** Have students post on their blogs, create videos, and issue frequent status reports.

If you want to engage students, find ways to make your curriculum relevant. A great way to do this is to have kids apply class concepts to their lives.

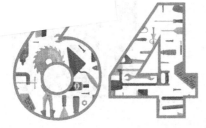

FASCINATE WITH THE FIRST FIVE

THE PROBLEM: TEACHERS UNDERESTIMATE THE ENGAGEMENT POWER OF THE FIRST FIVE MINUTES

IN THE *EDUTOPIA* article, "Your Lesson's First Five Minutes: Make Them Grand," Dr. Richard Curwin compares the first portion of class to a TV show or book. If the viewer or reader isn't engaged quickly, she'll change the channel or put the book back on the shelf. Dr. Curwin's argument is solid. Engage them with something entertaining, funny, inspiring, challenging, thought provoking, or fascinating as soon as the bell stops ringing. Visit Image 64.1 to peruse Dr. Curwin's article.

Image 64.1

THE HACK: USE THE FIRST FIVE TO CHALLENGE KIDS, BUILD RELATIONSHIPS, OR BOTH!

An engaging first five doesn't have to be an academic challenge. It's an amazing opportunity for bonding with students. Engage them with stories. These stories could be personal, humorous, interesting, or inspirational. They could be about you, something you witnessed, something you read, or saw on TV. Or simply ask for student input on personal matters:

- What do you think I should get my wife for our anniversary?

- What kind of car should I buy?

- I need a new workout. What would you suggest?

- What should I make my friend for his birthday dinner?

- What's a great date night movie?

A wonderful option is an academic application challenge:

- If you teach English, write a wordy paragraph, distribute it to students, and direct them to eliminate as many words as possible while maintaining the paragraph's flow and meaning.

- If you teach social studies, challenge kids to find an online original source about the day's lesson.

- If you teach biology, have students take their pulse. Prompt them to quickly research healthy heart rate ranges. Ask them to take it again. If it has changed, challenge them to speculate why.

I'm starting a unit on Mesoamerica. Here's tomorrow's first five discussion prompt:

Was Christopher Columbus a hero or a villain?

Another option is an anticipation prompt:

Charles Darwin observed various kinds of finches on the Galapagos Islands. What do you think he did next?

The first five minutes of class set the tone for the remainder of the class. Engage them initially and they'll be yours for the next fifty minutes.

WHAT YOU CAN DO TOMORROW

- **Tell a personal story.** Personal stories make you more approachable.

- **Invite a student to tell a story.** It could be a report on an important school event. It could be an important life achievement. Students will feel valued and they'll gain insight into peers.

- **Express enthusiasm.** A simple but powerful tool is to demonstrate enthusiasm for the day's lesson.

- **Compose and assign a Google Form that has a thought-provoking prompt.** Stir up a little controversy about the day's lesson.

Social Studies

- **Challenge students to practice an advanced skill, make a pre-diction, or solve a problem or mystery.** Consider the examples from above and apply them to your curriculum.
- **Alternate daily.** On Monday, do an academic challenge. On Tuesday, do something that helps you bond with students.

The first five minutes of class are crucial to student engagement. Use this time to bond with kids and challenge them.

HACK

GIVE STUDENTS VIRTUALLY NO INSTRUCTIONS

THE PROBLEM: TEACHERS TALK TOO MUCH AND ROB STUDENTS OF POWERFUL LEARNING OPPORTUNITIES

UNFORTUNATELY, MANY TEACHERS still embrace the stand-and-deliver model. They hover in front of disengaged youngsters, talking and talking and then talking some more. It's part of many instructors' DNA to feel the need to explain. By default, we want to elaborate and make sure we're completely understood. When we're asked a question, we're hardwired to answer thoroughly. But these very tendencies may be robbing kids of valuable learning opportunities. There's still a need for explanation; there's still a place for presentation; there's still room for inspirational messages.

> **These conversations were not just enjoyable, but unveiled a deep evolving understanding that probably would not have been present if I'd relied on the old stand-and-deliver method.**

Teachers should play these roles and display these skills, but the lion's share of class time should be devoted to student-led learning. Instructors who buck this trend are on the wrong side of history.

THE HACK: GIVE YOUR STUDENTS VIRTUALLY NO INSTRUCTIONS

Picture this…tomorrow you stroll confidently into your first-period class. You gleefully announce the day's essential question. You observe with satisfaction the looks on thirty adolescent faces as their intellectual gears perk to life and start rotating. You then point out that five minutes of the class are already in the rearview mirror, so they better get cracking! You spend the remainder of the period gliding from group to group – challenging, inspiring, coaching, offering new perspectives, evaluating, and congratulating. This, my dear friends, is the classroom of the future.

The great thing about this approach is that it can be used in any discipline. On the *Hacking Engagement Podcast*, I interview a lot of my students. One teacher frequently comes up in my conversations with these youngsters: Charlie Smith. Charlie teaches physics. His students often compliment his empowering teaching style. He issues a problem, then students work in small groups to create and evaluate solutions. Aim your QR code reader at Image 65.1 to hear Charlie and me discuss his teaching technique.

Image 65.1

Here's what Charlie inspired me to do the next day in my World Civ class. We were working through a unit on contemporary Asian issues, preparing to dive into the murky, dangerous, and confusing Korean dilemma. Instead of standing in front of my kids and presenting a lecture on Korean history, Charlie inspired me to ask a provocative question:

> You're the President of the United States. You must decide what to do about an increasingly hostile North Korea. If war breaks out in Korea, tens of millions of people, including thousands of American soldiers, could be dead within an hour. What will you do?

After issuing this prompt, some students panicked. "I don't know anything about Korea," they chorused. The old me would have launched into a passionate lecture about Korean history. The new me, however, knew that this was a golden teachable moment. I suggested a few outstanding web resources, but I also urged kids to find and then use their own resources, both human and technological. I pointed out that their classmates are wonderful problem-solvers and they should tap me only after they've exhausted their groupmates. It was magical. I cruised around the room, engaging with individuals and groups. These conversations were not just enjoyable, but unveiled a deep evolving understanding that probably would not have been present if I'd relied on the old stand-and-deliver method.

WHAT YOU CAN DO TOMORROW

- **Create a provocative prompt.** This is your essential question or questions. Design it in a provocative way, such as my example with Korea.

- **Challenge students to offer solutions.** This may not be easy for students. They're accustomed to having teachers provide them with information and solutions. Forcing kids to investigate in a deep way won't necessarily come naturally to them, but be patient. They'll get better with practice.

- **Encourage students to test their creations.** After kids come up with solutions, they must evaluate them. Please inspire students to make alterations to their solutions in the face of objective analysis.

- **Encourage students to evaluate other students' solutions.** This additional step will offer new perspectives and inspire future collaboration.

- **Conduct a whole-class discussion or debriefing.** This is where lively debate and deep learning can materialize.

Self-directed learning is the way of the future. Embrace this paradigm and grow your students into independent problem-solvers.

HACK

APPLY THE *YOU Y'ALL WE* TEMPLATE

THE PROBLEM: TEACHERS NEED AN ENGAGING GO-TO TEMPLATE THAT CAN BE APPLIED TO ANY LESSON

"*P*UT YOUR HAND *on a hot stove for a minute, and it will seem like an hour. Sit with a pretty girl, and an hour seems like a minute. That's relativity.*"
– ALBERT EINSTEIN

This wonderful quote is the embodiment of engagement. As teachers, we need to be more like the pretty companion (obviously not in terms of physical attraction) and less like the stove. Unfortunately, many educators are stuck in an unengaging routine. They stand and deliver content to an audience that is only partially engaged. A solid way to avoid becoming the interminable red glowing element on Einstein's stove is to use a battle-tested engagement template.

THE HACK: APPLY THE *YOU Y'ALL WE* TEMPLATE

I was recently exposed to a marvelous book by Norman Eng called *Teaching College: The Ultimate Guide to Lecturing, Presenting, and Engaging Students.* An essential portion of Norman's book is the promotion of Magdalene Lampert's engagement template: *You Y'all We.* Image 66.1 goes directly to Norman's book on Amazon.

Image 66.1

I was so taken by Norman's promotion of Dr. Lampert's template, and his directions on how to apply it, that I interviewed him on my podcast! After many years of being an instructor, Norman decided the traditional lesson template needed an upgrade. He is not alone in this thinking; in fact, I consider him a kindred spirit because I've gone through a similar metamorphosis. Here's the traditional lesson plan template that I've applied countless times in my career:

1. **I do…** the instructor demonstrates something.

2. **We do…** students apply the knowledge or skill in groups.

3. **You do…** students independently tackle an assignment or assessment.

The *You Y'all We* template shuffles this worn-out deck of cards:

1. **You…** students are immediately challenged to contemplate, offer solutions, wonder, apply, speculate, and compare and contrast.

2. **Y'all…** after students have taken the plunge independently, they collaborate with classmates.

3. **We…** once their adolescent wheels are spinning, they're ready for a whole-class discussion, debriefing, or perhaps some direct instruction.

WHAT YOU CAN DO TOMORROW

- **Issue an engaging hook for students to work on individually (You).** Examples:
  - You're introducing variables in algebra, so you prompt: *Describe when you solved a mystery. How did you do it? What were some serious obstacles?*
  - You're beginning a unit on *Catcher in the Rye* in English, so you prompt: *Describe what you miss most about being a little kid. How is being older frustrating? Would you like to go back for one day?*
  - You're delving into plate tectonics in earth science, so you prompt: *Describe the heaviest thing you've moved. How did you do it? What were some serious obstacles?*

- You're introducing flexibility in your health and PE class, so you prompt: *Describe a law or a school policy that needs to be eliminated or updated. Why does it need to change? What will happen if it doesn't?*

- **Challenge students to discuss their responses in small groups (Y'all).** It's been my experience that students are far more willing to share once they've had time to process an idea.

- **Instigate a class discussion or debriefing (We).** After kids have had time to reflect and collaborate, their participation levels will improve dramatically.

- **Dive into the lecture, the reading, and the lesson activities (We).**

Open Image 66.2 to hear my discussion with Norman Eng about this transformational template.

Apply the *You Y'all We* template over and over again, and watch student engagement and participation flourish.

Image 66.2

HACK

DANGLE A DILEMMA

THE PROBLEM: YOU'RE INVESTED IN YOUR LESSON, BUT YOUR STUDENTS AREN'T

ADOLF HITLER SENT Reinhard Heydrich to Czechoslovakia in 1941. His mission was to brutally stifle any Czech dissent to Nazi rule. He carried out his duties with ruthless precision. A handful of amazingly brave members of the Czech Resistance responded by assassinating Heydrich in the late spring of 1942. In retaliation, Hitler unleashed hell on Czechoslovakia.

Does this sound like a fascinating lesson? I certainly thought so. I sauntered into class and immediately started dishing out some knowledge. I was confident that I could grab students by their virtual lapels and pull them in. I treated them to some primary sources, my rendition of the assassination, movie clips from *Anthropoid* (the 2016 movie about the incident), and some thought-provoking prompts. The lesson went well, but not as well as I had hoped. History students sometimes grow numb when learning about yet another senseless mass slaughter. Something was missing from my lesson. Fortunately, my next class was a day behind. This afforded me with the opportunity to find the missing ingredient. On my drive home from school it hit me: *My students couldn't relate to the heart-wrenching choice the brave Czech assassins had to make.* I knew exactly what to do.

THE HACK: STOKE STUDENT ANTICIPATION BY DANGLING A DILEMMA

Obviously, your humble narrator is big on enthralling lesson hooks. A number of hacks in this book are devoted to just that. This hack will focus specifically on the power of presenting kids with a thorny dilemma. Such a dilemma offers immediate relevancy. The student is shoved into the lesson! Kids strolled into my class the next day, thinking, "I wonder what they're serving for lunch?" when suddenly – I dropped a dilemma prompt that deposited them into the bleak and terrifying world of Nazi-occupied Prague. Dilemmas are all about trade-offs. Frequently, there are no good answers, just painful, or ultra painful, courses. Here's the dilemma I created for students for the Heydrich Assassination Lesson:

> Our town is occupied by a horribly abusive foreign government. You join the resistance. You have a chance to kill an official who's responsible for the deaths of many students at our school. But, if you kill this evil man, the reprisals will be devastating! First on the execution list will be your friends and family. Do you pull the trigger?

Such a dilemma forces students into the lesson. They began to feel like a Czech resistance fighter confronted with an agonizing choice.

Instructors in non-humanities curriculums often complain that dilemma questions are easy to create in history or English class, but not so easy to concoct in math and science. But please consider just some of the gut-wrenching dilemmas that scientists have faced:

- Copernicus' struggles with the church due to his proposal that the sun was the center of the universe, not the earth.

- The Malthusian Trap and the theory that population growth is ahead of agricultural growth, so the food supply will become inadequate.

- Einstein's letter to Roosevelt, warning about atomic bombs and advocating that the U.S. should start its own nuclear program, which led to the Manhattan Project.

- Scientific experiments or tests on animals, forcing them to undergo pain, suffering, distress, or death.

- The Chaos Theory, the branch of mathematics that deals with nonlinear things that are difficult to predict or control, like weather, the stock market, turbulence, or brain states.

Math involves data. Application of data can lead to incredibly provocative dilemmas. This one ignites high schoolers' passions:

The Centers for Disease Control and Prevention released data demonstrating that sixteen- and seventeen-year-old drivers are three times more likely to wreck than eighteen- and nineteen-year-olds. Should the driving age be eighteen?

Image 67.1

Hear a pair of my brilliant students advocate for engaging hooks in Image 67.1.

WHAT YOU CAN DO TOMORROW

- **Create a hook dilemma for tomorrow's lesson.** If you're having a hard time coming up with one, search online. You can Google "classic dilemmas" and then see if you can apply one, or morph one, for tomorrow's lesson.

- **Challenge students to think about the dilemma.** Project a Google Stopwatch and give them a minute to think about their responses.

- **Break students into small groups and encourage them to share their thoughts.** Count down three minutes on the Google Stopwatch while you circulate around the room listening, participating, and if needed, prodding.

- **Debrief kids.** Allow students to spout some ideas, or challenge conventional thinking.

Before you know it, students will be eagerly anticipating your lessons and the opportunity to debate topics such as whether they would have murdered Baby Hitler.

HACK

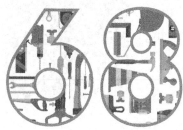

INSPIRE 100% PARTICIPATION IN YOUR NEXT CLASS DISCUSSION

THE PROBLEM: A LIMITED NUMBER OF STUDENTS PARTICIPATE IN CLASS DISCUSSIONS

THE NEXT THREE hacks show how to up the engagement level for your next class discussion, starting with participation. I once worked with a talented student teacher. I watched him interact with students in an advanced-level class discussion, and the topic was probed in depth. My student teacher and his fellow yakkers were engaged and animated. He was pretty pumped after class, till I rained on his parade. The problem with the discussion was that it was conducted between my student teacher and only a handful of students. The other kids, while initially engaged, were lost through attrition. Being a cooperating teacher affords an interesting perspective. I stealthily watched students systematically check out of the convo and start fidgeting. I reassured my disappointed young protégé that successful veteran instructors also struggle with comprehensive engagement and participation in class discussion. I certainly have. We became determined to undermine this status quo.

THE HACK: USE TECHNOLOGY TO ENTICE EVEN THE SHYEST OF SHY TO PARTICIPATE

Mark Barnes has a solution to this specific and significant problem. He's absolutely certain teachers can manifest 100% student participation in class discussion. Picture a discussion where the shy kids, the quiet kids, the kids who are too cool, the sarcastic kids, and even the kids who are struggling with skills and content – all contribute.

Image 68.1

In the *Hack Learning Podcast* episode on class participation, Mark promotes using technology to entice student participation. Hear Mark's ideas by opening the QR code in Image 68.1.

Any of these tools will create an irresistible conversational environment:

- TodaysMeet
- Padlet
- Twitter
- Voxer

With the exception of Voxer, these tools act like virtual bulletin boards. You can see everyone who's participating. Don't worry; kids will want to post. They'll start seeing their peers' posts and be powerfully compelled. The cool thing about Voxer is the ability to create sub-discussion groups of up to fifteen students, where students can actually talk instead of type. The same accountability factor is still present. Students who vox will have a virtual verbal footprint in the conversation; those who don't contribute will not.

For his next classroom discussion, my student teacher posed a question on a Padlet virtual bulletin board. An avalanche of posts and replies ensued! For the subsequent discussion, he created a hashtag chat and students tweeted their views for all to read. At the end of the semester, he left my tutelage well-equipped to ensure student participation in future classrooms. The experience also left me, his mentor, with a solution to a puzzle that had always dogged me.

WHAT YOU CAN DO TOMORROW

- **Decide on a platform.** Any of the choices listed in this hack will work. Tinker with each and see which resonates with you.

- **Describe the platform to students.** My experience has been that kids catch on pretty fast.

- **Encourage participation with two simple guidelines.** This probably won't be necessary because students will want to participate, but tell them you want to hear or read everyone's views. Mark Barnes encouraged each student to post one original thought and then reply to at least one classmate. And finally, have students take ownership over their comments by signing their names.

- **Discuss appropriate use.** Remind students of all the things you've hopefully discussed all year about being good digital citizens.

- **Teachers need to talk too.** This is a class discussion. You're part of the class. You can inspire participation with strategic posts and replies.

Old-school class discussions exclude students. Use technology to foster 100% participation.

HACK

SHOVE YOUR NEXT CLASS DISCUSSION ON TO THE TWITTERSPHERE

THE PROBLEM: YOUR CLASS DISCUSSIONS NEED AN INFUSION OF ENERGY

OUR GOAL AS educators should be to get all students participating in class discussions, and to facilitate passionate discourse and inquiry. In my first book and on my podcast, I frequently promote Socratic seminars. I love Socratic seminars because they provide a template to make your engaging class discussion dreams come true. The next two hacks will provide you with novel ways to evolve Socratic seminars. These tactics will infuse a jolt of energy to an already solid class activity.

THE HACK: MIGRATE YOUR SOCRATIC SEMINAR TO TWITTER

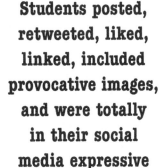

Students posted, retweeted, liked, linked, included provocative images, and were totally in their social media expressive comfort zone.

Last semester was winding down and I needed to include one more Socratic seminar on an important topic. We had done a number of Socratic seminars during the semester. The energy had been there in the beginning, but started to wane a bit as the semester drew to a close. I decided to reignite engagement by morphing our last seminar into a Twitter chat. I became familiar with Twitter chats after I was asked to moderate one after the publication of my first book. I logged into the chat and I was quickly overwhelmed. I was being required to multitask at what seemed an Olympic pace. As soon as I would read an interesting tweet, I would try to compose a response, include a link and an image, retweet and hit like, all before another wave of tweets descended, making my responses old news. I didn't enjoy the hyper nature of the format. I was reluctant to be involved in another Twitter chat.

But then I learned about TweetDeck, which allows you to schedule your tweets.

Image 69.1

Image 69.2

You can include links and images, and schedule a time to post it. And then like magic, your tweet materializes at 8:33 a.m. on September 14. I was asked to moderate another Twitter chat, but this time, I was ready. I scheduled sixteen tweets in the thirty-minute window. As the chat progressed, I casually responded to the tweets I found compelling, while my tweets unfolded right on schedule. It was beautiful! Follow the code in Image 69.1 directly to TweetDeck.

Of course, I immediately started to scheme as to how I could make my last Socratic seminar a Twitter chat. It was held on a Sunday evening, and it was a roaring success. Students posted, retweeted, liked, linked, included provocative images, and were totally in their social media expressive comfort zone. Please try this! Your students will love it. Please open Image 69.2 to hear one of my fantastic students advocate for the class Twitter chat.

WHAT YOU CAN DO TOMORROW

- **Expose students to TweetDeck.** Many won't recognize it, but they'll master it rapidly. Have them practice scheduling some tweets.

- **Create a chat hashtag.** We use #heywc1, as in, *Hey, World Civilization 1!* All tweets must include your created tag in order to be seen.

- **Designate the chat time.** We conducted our chat from 7:30 to 8:30 p.m. on a Sunday. A few students were busy, but thanks to TweetDeck, they were able to schedule their tweets and participate like they were camped out in front of their monitors.

- **Preview the Socratic seminar prompts and when they'll appear.** At 7:31 p.m., Question 1 will appear. At 7:36, Question 2 will appear. I had five questions nicely spaced. This gave students the opportunity to think about great

responses and schedule them. You can set aside some class time for kids to schedule their tweets in TweetDeck.

• **Invite VIPs to participate.** Ask your district administrators to jump in.

Twitter is a fact of modern life. Embrace it and all its potential to engage your students in discussion.

HACK

PULL UP A PHILOSOPHICAL CHAIR

THE PROBLEM: A FEW STUDENTS DOMINATE DISCUSSIONS, WHILE OTHERS SIT IN SILENCE

As a teacher, you've probably thought: *Well, I certainly know Maria and Myles' views, but I have no idea about David and Russell's positions.* Of course you can't count a discussion as truly engaging for the class if it only engages a handful of students. It's common to have a few extroverted students dominate class discussion.

The cliché, *They voted with their feet,* rather charmingly and beautifully describes a situation where reserved people make their feelings known through some type of action or movement. This hack will empower reserved students to open their mouths, and if they don't opt to be verbal, they can at least vote with their feet.

THE HACK: TACKLE A THORNY DILEMMA WITH PHILOSOPHICAL CHAIRS

Philosophical Chairs combines two of my favorite activities: scholarship and movement. This solid tactic will coax wallflowers out of the shadows! A big mistake that many non-humanities teachers make is not recognizing the epic potential that debate could have in math, science, or health class. Applications for history or ELA curriculums are obvious, but let's get our math and science students yakking too.

I challenged kids to evaluate a letter composed by Lin Zexu in 1839. The exasperated Chinese official wrote Queen Elizabeth begging her to halt the British opium trade. This was a wonderful provocative subject for our session. This tactic could be employed in any class where students are presented with a problem or a dilemma and are asked to create solutions, and then are required to evaluate and defend choices and options. Hmm! That sounds like what all teachers, regardless of the subject, should strive for frequently.

Philosophical Chairs, like Socratic seminars, offers a structured template which facilitates enthusiastic participation. Teachers place the following signs around their rooms:

- *YES* on the left wall

- *NO* on the right wall

- *UNDECIDED* on the back wall

Image 70.1

Image 70.2

In a Philosophical Chairs session, challenging prompts are issued by the moderator. If students believe the answer is YES, they cruise over to the left side of the room and start promoting. Classmates listen to peers' views and then migrate to portions of the room that represent their endorsement of, or rejection of, the messages that outspoken colleagues have tossed out. What's cool is that kids can migrate at any time. If a classmate makes a great point, they gather their things and shuffle off to another portion of the room. Everyone is free to move, even students who are bellowing certainty. If they rethink their views in light of new evidence or perspectives, it's time to rent a virtual U-Haul. You can even add some drama. Show kids proceedings of the British House of Commons. When parliamentarians hear something awesome, they don't just nod politely, they bust out a joyous, "HEAR…HEAR…HEAR!" Follow the code in Image 70.1 to access a wonderful video that will demonstrate Philosophical Chairs in action.

Image 70.2 will lead you to the Stanford History Education Group. SHEG provides teachers with wonderful primary sources. When they are accompanied by student activities, they will guarantee deep understanding and set up your Philosophical Chairs perfectly.

And finally, hear my discussion with Joel Breakstone of the Stanford History Education Group, in Image 70.3. We talk a lot about Philosophical Chairs.

Image 70.3

WHAT YOU CAN DO TOMORROW

- **Watch the Teaching Channel video on Philosophical Chairs.** This video (accessible in Image 70.3) does a marvelous job of describing and demonstrating the process.

- **Designate preparation materials.** If you teach in the humanities, please check out the Stanford History Education Group. Their primary source packets are perfect for Philosophical Chairs prep.

- **Arrange your room.** Perhaps divide the desks into three large groups. Orient one group to the left (YES), one to the right (NO), and one to the back (UNDECIDED). Clear the middle of the room because it's going to be as busy as a traffic intersection.

- **Create provocative prompts.** Create at least three higher-level thinking prompts that force students to make choices. For a recent Philosophical Chairs, I prompted, *Was Gandhi's non-violent campaign in India a success?* On the face of it, it would seem yes, but as soon as India got its independence, terrible violence broke out between Hindus and Muslims that resulted in the violent partition of the subcontinent. It was a complicated and provocative prompt. Those are the types of questions you want to ask.

Philosophical Chairs creates a template and an atmosphere where engaging class discussion materializes, and transforms all kids into participants, even if they're just voting with their feet.

HACK

MORPH STUDENT IDENTITIES

THE PROBLEM: YOUR *GO-TO* LEARNING ACTIVITY NEEDS AN UPGRADE

IT'S NO SECRET by now that I'm a Socratic seminar guy. They're the embodiment of self-directed learning and student collaboration. Kids take a complex topic, learn about it, and then sit in a circle with their peers and apply it, discuss it, debate it, explain it, and ask questions of one another. My experience has been that concepts, events, and topics covered in this fashion lead to deep understanding and significant engagement. But everything, even things you and your students love, will get old if you don't alter it occasionally.

I faced this dilemma in teaching the incredibly complex topic of the Syrian Civil War. I wanted students to engage in a Socratic seminar, but I wanted it to be different. We had conducted a number of such seminars and I felt the format was getting a bit stale. I decided that in order for my students to understand the Syrian Civil War, they needed to become the powerful actors involved.

THE HACK: MORPH STUDENT IDENTITIES FOR YOUR NEXT SOCRATIC SEMINAR

There's certainly nothing new about role playing or simulations, but they can add a new engaging twist when applied to your next Socratic seminar. For my Syrian Civil War seminar, students were required to assume the persona of a leader of one of these ten nations or entities:

1. Iran

2. Iraq

3. ISIS

4. Israel

5. Palestinians

6. Russia

7. Saudi Arabia

8. Syria

9. Turkey

10. United States

Students prepped in the typical way, but in this case they also prepped from the perspective of their adopted nations or groups. Yes…some students were forced to advocate for ISIS. They did a remarkable job! Please don't worry. None of them became an ISIS recruit, or a war bride. Advocating for a position you find abhorrent leads to deep understanding. Not only did kids do a fine job prepping, they also embraced their characters. I witnessed a student do a powerful impersonation of Donald Trump. I had no idea whether this young person was a fan of the president, or not. Based on his performance, it seemed like he was a fan.

Image 71.1

During our discussion after the seminar, it became clear that his opinion toward Donald Trump was conflicted. Yet his performance was so compelling, you'd never have guessed his true feelings. But please understand, kids don't have to be dramatic. One student surprised his peers by uttering anti-Semitic remarks. He didn't speak dramatically, but in a cold, calculating way. Many kids were taken aback until after the seminar when he explained that he was portraying the leader of Iran, who has said many such things.

Consider how these two interesting performances inspired wonder: *Why is he saying those awful things? Why is he acting like that?* These questions were addressed later, but such thoughts percolated in kids' minds as the seminar unfolded. Access Image 71.1 to hear two passionate testimonials from my students.

WHAT YOU CAN DO TOMORROW

- **Settle on a topic.** Consider the unit you're currently teaching. Make a list of big concepts you want students to grasp in a deep fashion. Choose one that could lead to a passionate debate, is quite complex, or is both provocative and complex (like my example of the Syrian Civil War).

- **List the important players.** These are the people or entities your students will portray in the seminar. You don't have to come up with ten. If you have a smaller number, you can have two or more students represent the same person or group.

- **Assign student roles.** This can be done randomly, or instructors can assign roles opposite of what students would choose. This is a great intellectual challenge because it forces kids to advocate for positions they dislike.

- **Prompt kids to research.** An essential aspect of the Socratic seminar experience is self-directed learning. Create provocative questions that will foster passionate research. These questions will be addressed during the seminar.

- **Encourage students TO BE their roles.** Challenge kids to dress the part, act the part, be passionate, and even dramatic in order to fully embrace their assigned viewpoints.

Socratic seminars are wonderful learning experiences. Keep them fresh and engaging by forcing kids to be somebody they are not!

HACK

DETONATE THE BORING GUEST SPEAKER TEMPLATE

THE PROBLEM: MANY GUEST PRESENTATIONS DON'T ENGAGE STUDENTS

ABOUT A DECADE ago, I was asked to present to college education majors. I was really pumped and figured I'd lay down some indispensable knowledge. I stepped into that classroom raring to go. Fifty minutes later, I was still talking! I looked at the clock and realized that I was five minutes from the finish line. I asked if there were any questions. I was greeted with stony silence. I repeated my plea, only to witness many students gathering their things, standing up, and heading toward the exit. A few audience members stopped by and thanked me and said they enjoyed my presentation, but I sensed that I bored many of the students and they were glad I was done.

Today when I'm invited to college classes – which I dearly love – I present in fifteen-minute segments. I build-in audience hands-on application and reflection activities. My presentations are *doing* experiences, not *sitting and listening* experiences. I savor many post-presentation questions that often turn into fascinating discussions. I'm often greeted and thanked warmly as students exit. I've learned the hard way how to be an engaging guest presenter, and I now love conducting Professional Development classes in particular.

It's totally in your power to make guest presentations engaging.

THE HACK: PREP FOR A GREAT GUEST PRESENTATION THE DAY BEFORE

I get why guest presenters often embark on marathon blabfests. They've been invited to share their knowledge, but they don't know your students. Many have never taught. Many deal with adults all day. Kids are different! Sadly, many students and remarkably many teachers look at guest presenter day as a day off. *I can take it easy today and let someone else teach my class*; this is an unfortunate attitude.

Instead, help your guest. Prime the pump with your students. I've been on both sides of the presentation coin. I know how helpful it is if students have some accountability. It's totally in your power to make guest presentations engaging. Embrace this mantra:

> I'm going to plan, prepare my students, have them create questions the day prior, hold them accountable, build significant anticipation, and then once the presentation starts, stay active and participate.

An amazing classroom presentation is forged the day before your guest's visit.

WHAT YOU CAN DO TOMORROW

- **Prepare a handout with vital background information.** Make certain your students know about your guest. This busy person is volunteering his time to help your students grow. Promote the guest the day before with a bio and describe his accomplishments. Your students will be more receptive from the start.

- **Distribute a question template.** Hold students accountable by taking class time the day before to brainstorm questions for the presenter. Provide incentives for students to ask questions early and often. The "Does anyone have any questions?" prompt at the end is not engaging.

- **Brainstorm activities with the presenter.** Actively plan together. You know what engages your students, so suggest activities that can be done at various junctures. Hands-on application activities are particularly powerful. I've found that the more involved I am in the planning phase, the better.

- **On presentation day, have each student greet and shake hands with the presenter on their way into class.** This is

a wonderful tip which enhances everyone's comfort leve
Students are more apt to ask questions, and guests feel more
at ease.

- **After the presentation, pass around a thank-you note.** This is
a formative assessment. Ask students to include a message
about why they enjoyed the presentation.

Guest presentations can be wonderful and engaging. It's up to the teacher to make them that way.

HACK

LISTEN TO STUDENTS
WITH YOUR ENTIRE BODY

THE PROBLEM: TEACHERS GET DISTRACTED
AND DON'T LISTEN TO STUDENTS

Does your school day sometimes resemble an assembly line? Mine has. Some days I feel like I process, instead of engage, one hundred and fifty students. Some days, kids just seem to come at me in waves. They're like a blur. I'm not proud to confess this, but on a few rare occasions, on particularly frazzled days, a student has attempted to engage me and I haven't given them my undivided attention. Guilty! If you're not engaged with students, they sure as shootin' won't be engaged with you.

Which is why a recent Voxer chat with a veteran comrade inspired me. Liz Galarza teaches writing to sixth-graders in Bayshore, New York. She spent her early years, however, teaching in the South Bronx. She knows about engaging students in challenging settings. When I

Students who don't sense you're listening will not feel valued.

prompted her about engagement, she responded with one powerful sentence: "Really listen to your students." I love Liz's simple and profound directive. But, really listening does not just mean with your ears, or even just with your head. To really listen, use your entire body.

THE HACK: USE YOUR ENTIRE BODY TO SHOW STUDENTS YOU'RE LISTENING

In the process of writing my first book, I did a lot of research on nonverbal communication. *The Definitive Book of Body Language* by Barbara and Allan Pease is, quite frankly, one of the most enjoyable books I've read. Point your QR code reader on Image 73.1 to go directly to the book on Amazon.

Image 73.1

We communicate a lot more than simply our words. My objective was to become a more effective nonverbal listener. And I let my students in on the game. We spent the better part of a grading period evaluating each other's body language. They'd totally bust me if I didn't listen to them with my feet, legs, arms, hands, body position, head movements, and my expressions. They had a blast. I had a blast. We all learned to be better nonverbal listeners. Here are the stated objectives that I shared with my students:

- My feet indicate where I really want to go. If I'm interacting with a student while standing, I'll make certain to point my feet directly at them.

- If I expose my palms to a student, it'll help put her at ease. She'll also know that I'm not carrying any weapons.

- If I fold my arms tightly across my body, or cross my legs to the point where they look like a twisted rope, I'm not transmitting open listening signals. (This one is hard to remember in Ohio, in January, when the outdoor temp is six degrees.)

- I'll strive to maintain eye contact and nod slowly when I understand.

- I'll try to match my expressions with my communication partner. If I want to reassure, I'll smile. If it's a serious conversation, I'll focus my eyes and keep nodding.

- Finally, I'll have some fun! I'll show a kid I'm really engaged by mirroring his body language. If he's sitting with his legs crossed, I'll cross my legs. If she leans toward me, I'll lean toward her. If he puts his chin on his fist, I'll put my chin on my fist. This is also an awesome tactic to use with your significant other.

WHAT YOU CAN DO TOMORROW

- **Practice on your significant other or family member.** You prepare for class at home. Why not become a better nonverbal listener at home, too?

- **Enlighten students about your goal.** Let your students in on your objective to become a better nonverbal listener. This will be a lot of fun and will put active nonverbal listening on everyone's radar. Who knows…in your quest to become an active nonverbal listener, you may just create thirty disciples.

- **Play an active listening game.** Have students pair up and take turns describing an experience to one another. Once the interaction concludes, instruct the talking student to record observations about the listener's nonverbal signals.

- **Have student performers demonstrate effective nonverbal listening techniques.** Have small groups of students role-play each of the nonverbal listening bullets.

- **Practice nonverbal listening in one-on-one interactions.** Encourage conversations with students where you can consciously practice listening with your entire body.

Students who don't sense you're listening will not feel valued. Work on your nonverbal listening skills to engage kids, and teach them the same skills.

HACK

SOLVE A PUZZLE WITH EDPUZZLE

THE PROBLEM: SOME STUDENTS SLACK WITH FLIPPED LEARNING

OKAY, HERE'S MY problem. In my World Civilization class, all my lectures are flipped. My students are remarkably complimentary of this delivery method. I feel like my recorded lectures are far superior to my live performances. I guess that's why I always give a thumbs-down to Pandora's live tracks; they're just not quite as smooth as the recorded versions.

I wasn't certain, however, that students were watching my flipped presentations in their entirety. After all, one could copy lecture notes from a peer. That's not being engaged; that's being a slacker. I didn't think it happened a lot, but I was certain it happened some. Also, I felt a bit disconnected because kids watched my flipped lectures outside of class. I wanted my students' flipped presentation experience to be more collaborative and engaging.

Image 74.1

When I'm stumped, I ask for help. For a more engaging flipped presentation quest, I consulted Jennifer Gonzalez's magnificent book, *The Teacher's Guide to Tech*. This downloadable resource is updated yearly. The version I'm consulting contains one hundred and thirty tech tools. I can't wait to see what's added next year! Jennifer's book contains a section on flipped instruction. I found my solution in minutes! Learn more about Jennifer's book via Image 74.1.

Image 74.2

THE HACK: TRANSFORM YOUR FLIPPED PRESENTATION WITH EDPUZZLE

EDpuzzle is a remarkable free tool. You simply upload your flipped video and then strategically embed prompts. It reminds me of watching an on-demand program. Many cable providers will not allow you to fast-forward, so you must watch the commercials. You can set EDpuzzle so students can't fast-forward either! They must watch the segment and then respond to the prompt before moving on. The prompts can be multiple choice or extended response. Once kids have answered, they hit submit. Teachers can easily access student responses and see if the student even watched the video. It's a wonderful flipped presentation accountability tool, and it even works seamlessly with Google Classroom. This tool ultimately makes flipped learning more engaging, and it solved my issue perfectly. Follow Image 74.2 to the EDpuzzle site.

Image 74.3

Open Image 74.3 to listen to students endorse this cool tech tool.

WHAT YOU CAN DO TOMORROW

- **Create an EDpuzzle account.** EDpuzzle is free and you can use your Google login.

- **Upload a video.** Select CREATE and then NEW VIDEO or UPLOAD VIDEO. EDpuzzle has a vast library to choose from, or you can upload your own YouTube video.

- **Insert questions using EDpuzzle.** Once you've decided on a video, select the USE IT option. Then drag the green question mark to where you want to insert questions. Type the question, save your work, and you're good to go!

- **Publish to Google Classroom or copy the link**. After your work is saved, select FINISH. EDpuzzle gives you the option of posting on your Google Classroom, or distributing the link.

- **Review student responses.** Select the PROGRESS option on the right-hand side of any assignment. All your students will be listed. You'll see whether they've completed the presentation and you can also review their responses.

Use EDpuzzle to banish slacking, and add accountability and collaboration to flipped presentations.

HACK

PURGE PRESENTATION PREDICTABILITY WITH PEAR DECK

THE PROBLEM: TEACHER PRESENTATIONS NEED TO BE MORE ENGAGING

IN THE PREVIOUS hack, I promoted the idea of flipping your lectures and then enhancing engagement, collaboration, and accountability with EDpuzzle. This tactic works splendidly with assigned videos. But live teacher presentations need engagement levers as well!

THE HACK: EMBED TANTALIZING BOOKS AND PROVOCATIVE PROMPTS WITH PEAR DUCK

Even though much of my instruction is flipped, it's still important to frequently present in front of students. While my kids enjoy my recordings, periodically I treat

Morph your static sit-and-listen-fests into intense student collaboration-fests.

them to a live performance. My wife and I watched *Jersey Boys* on the big screen and then we saw it live on stage. There was no comparison. Sometimes, you have to go all Broadway on your kids. Sometimes, you need to be the sage on stage.

For engagement sake, I suggest keeping presentations relatively short. My self-imposed limit is ten minutes. Presentation length is crucial. Think about the science behind the TedTalk; they'll cut you off at eighteen minutes. Teachers need to be more Ted-like. Consider the template of this book: Each hack is roughly six hundred words and can be consumed quickly. The entire book is comprised of a little over thirty thousand words. Believe me, I could have written more, but my goal was to get to the point. Emulate this model in your presentations.

In addition to limiting the length of your presentation, drastically limit the amount of tedious text on each slide. Instead, populate them with compelling images. And here is where Pear Deck makes a dramatic appearance. Infuse your presentation with highly interactive engaging prompts by utilizing this amazing tool. Morph your static sit-and-listen-fests into intense student collaboration-fests. Transform your lectures into twenty-five separate and simultaneous student-teacher conversations. Pear Deck allows you to:

- Upload an existing presentation in Google Slides or PowerPoint.

- Invite students to follow your presentation on their devices, while you control the pace.

- Insert engaging prompts before and during your performance.

- Hide student responses until the teacher decides to display them, and student names may remain a mystery.

Image 75.1

This style of presentation is the future! Please give this outstanding engagement tool a try. Follow the code in Image 75.1 to the Pear Deck website.

After you've logged-in, access the short video tutorials. You'll have no problem figuring out how to use this tool. Please access Image 75.2 to listen to my description of how I use Pear Deck in my class.

Image 75.2

WHAT YOU CAN DO TOMORROW

- **Google search for Pear Deck tutorial videos.** You'll find plenty of short and informative choices. Like most online education tools, you can gain access to some awesome features if you pay. I have not done this because I'm still happy with the abilities of the free version.

- **Select or create a brief Google Slides or PowerPoint presentation.** I like to keep mine at less than ten slides. Please be careful of your presentation length.

- **Insert a fabulous hook into your first slide.** Dilemmas constitute great hooks. Consult Hack 67 for ideas.
- **Prompt students to respond through Pear Deck.** Display student responses once all kids have answered. Waiting to display anonymous responses will eliminate the peer-pressure factor. Include a multiple-choice prompt midway through the presentation, and a short answer or multiple-choice assessment question at the end.

Pear Deck creates a collaborative and engaging presentation environment. Embrace this new way to present and enthrall your kids.

HACK

AN INTENSE EXPERIENCE + BLOGGING = POWERFUL ENGAGEMENT

THE PROBLEM: YOUR BLOG PROMPTS NEED A BURST OF ENERGY

I'LL BET YOU remember bringing home one of your elementary school artistic masterpieces. Your mama probably made a big fuss and attached it to the fridge with magnets. You probably felt a real sense of pride.

Image 76.1

Now, picture your mom making a big fuss, then promptly taking your finger-paint masterpiece out into the backyard and burning it. This is exactly how we learned the profound concept of non-attachment in our unit on Buddhism in World Civilization. Image 76.1 will take you to my blog, where you can view the prompt, the mandala link, and some cool student creations (before they were burned!).

As an older guy, I get non-attachment. I observe my aging

face in the mirror every morning. I glance down at my withering skin. I always think, *How the hell did this happen?* Well, it is happening, but curiously it's still me, at least temporarily. Every cell in the body goes through a staggered destruction and creation process. No one is the same person he was a decade ago…literally! Over time, we are slowly forced into non-attachment of our younger selves. It's hard for young, supple, beautiful, bright-eyed, smooth-skinned seventeen-year-olds to grasp this concept.

THE HACK: CREATE A REAL-LIFE EXPERIENCE
THAT TEACHES AND ENGAGES

It's easy to find online video demonstrations of Buddhist monks circling around a mandala they have painstakingly created with grains of brightly colored sand. Their

final product never fails to mystify and amaze. And then, of course, they destroy it. By doing this, they detach from this beautiful object.

My artistic son David showed me a cool way to create a simplistic hand-drawn mandala with a square sheet of paper. Students can make them as elaborate as they please. Once completed, we hang the mandalas in the hallway for two days. It's fascinating to listen and observe my students showing peers their mandalas between classes. Invariably I see surprised faces when my students explain to their friends how we're going to burn them the next day. When peers challenge my students on this, I nearly do handsprings when I hear my students say, "I can't wait to burn mine. It's to show non-attachment." In Image 76.2, see Sami Rammelsberg getting ready to burn her mandala at the stake.

Students will remember this activity and its lessons about attachment for decades. Hopefully, it will help them in middle age when the aging process causes them to suffer.

Image 76.2

WHAT YOU CAN DO TOMORROW

- **Decide what's an essential concept in the unit you're studying.** Choose a topic that's important and elusive; in other words, students often struggle with it.

- **Survey your students.** Challenge kids to dream up a real-life experience demonstrating the concept. It should be something they can do individually, or as a class. If they don't come up with something awesome, then you might have to step in. But give them the first crack. They just might amaze you.

- **Unleash the experience.** My students burned then blogged. Students should act, then reflect and evaluate in some fashion.

Deep engagement is fostered by real-life application. Some of the best real-life experiences can be manufactured.

HACK

DRESS THE PART AND ENGAGE WITH THIS COOL OLD-SKOOL TOOL

THE PROBLEM: TEACHERS NEGLECT THE POWER OF COSTUME

IN 1984, I was a graduate student at Ohio State University. That was the year I decided to become a teacher. Also that year, ironically, the satire movie *Teachers* was filmed at Central High School in Columbus, Ohio. The movie paints a bleak and sarcastic portrait of American public education. One of the bizarre characters in *Teachers* was social studies teacher Herbert Gower, played by Richard Mulligan. He's a perfect role model for this hack. Mr. Gower, who had serious mental issues, had a knack for engaging slacker students. He frequently showed up to class in costume and in character. There's one iconic scene where Mr. Gower is dressed as George Washington, surrounded by students sitting in desks pretending they're rowing! His students were intensely engaged as they learned about America's hero crossing the Delaware.

Patty Thompson is a veteran middle school history teacher and a modern version of Mr. Gower. She says, "I'm always looking for something different to engage my students. My students love when I dress the part. It also engages me. I feel more authentic. When I walk into the room as Cleopatra, Medusa, or Athena, kids get really excited. I can see it in their eyes and their body language. There's also a huge uptick in student participation." I particularly loved Patty's response when I asked her why she started dressing up. "I used to be a preschool teacher. We always focused on fun and artistic creativity. That's the music of learning. That's the dance! I knew I had to bring some of that magic to older students."

THE HACK: DRESS LIKE SOMEONE YOU'RE STUDYING

This hack is simple. If you're studying Mark Twain, dress like him. If you want to make an impact about women's rights in the Islamic world, dress like Malala Yousafzai. It's engaging for kids; it's engaging for you.

Teachers, however, must be careful with this hack. If you're a dude, you should probably dress only as other males. Always dress school-appropriate. You may want to steer clear of wearing an outfit Josephine Baker would have worn on stage in Paris! You should never, in any way, shape, or form, alter your skin color, or wear wigs to appear like a member of a race different than your own. Just use some common sense and you'll be fine. I've dressed as Gandhi, even though I'm not an Indian. Of course, it helps that I look like Gandhi. I put on a white t-shirt, shorts, sandals, and wrapped a white sheet around my body like an Indian khadi. My students walked into class and found me seated on the floor. It was a lot of fun.

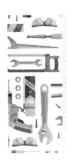

WHAT YOU CAN DO TOMORROW

- **Make a list of individuals who could make guest appearances.** Search the unit you're studying. Your list of potential impersonations might be pretty small, but all it takes is one.

- **Search your closet for clothing that could be used as a costume item.** Putting yourself in character may be as simple as putting on an army helmet. I used a white sheet to become Gandhi.

- **Check online for reasonably priced costumes.** If you're really serious, buy a costume. Patty Thompson decks out from head to toe. Send your principal the requisition.

- **Challenge students to participate.** Sponsor a student *Impersonate Your Favorite Scientist, Artist, Soldier, Author, or Civil Rights Leader Day*. Make certain to create clearly defined boundaries if you go this route.

Teachers have been engaging students with costumes for decades. This is a wonderful, low-tech way to enthrall students.

HACK

TRANSFORM YOUR CLASS INTO STUDENTS' FAVORITE SITCOM

THE PROBLEM: STUDENTS ENTER MANY CLASSROOMS WITH LITTLE TO NO JOY

I DEVOTED AN ENTIRE chapter of my previous book, *You've Gotta Connect,* to humor. This is a powerful tool that oozes engagement potential. You might be thinking, *I'm not a funny person.* But hey, you don't have to be a stand-up comedian. You can be the straight man. On my favorite sitcom, *The Office,* I'd much rather be the character Jim Halpert instead of Dwight Schrute or Michael Scott. The straight man is always much cooler and typically ends up with the girl. So relax, you can be the straight man. The goal is to welcome humor into your classroom, not to try to become something you're not, or damage your professional image.

Humor is incredibly engaging. Kids choose humor. Consider student-created skits and videos: Students typically put as much effort into making them funny as they do into satisfying the lesson prompt. Observe students in their natural habitat…surfing the internet. They'll watch one ridiculous video after another. Not many kids turn on a PBS documentary when they collapse on the couch after school. Instead of fighting this natural inclination, let's climb aboard the humor train.

Invite humor into your classroom and witness profound student enjoyment, which opens the door to greater engagement.

THE HACK: STRATEGICALLY INTRODUCE HUMOR

I'm devoted to incorporating humor in my classroom and it has paid huge dividends. After former students greet me, they usually follow with, "Do you remember the day…" These stories almost always have a humorous twist. Many teachers have discovered the amazing engagement potential of humor. Maurice Elias wrote an extremely popular piece for *Edutopia,* and the piece has a surprisingly pedestrian title: "Using Humor in the Classroom." Follow the QR code in Image 78.1 to read the article.

Image 78.1

Here are some ways you can remain the straight man, but still invite humor into your classroom:

- Tell a funny story about a mistake you made.

- Post a cartoon which reinforces your lesson.

- Share a funny news article.

- Show a hilarious YouTube video.

- Describe a dorky thing you did when you were your students' age.

- Show an image of your dog and what she did to make you laugh. *Google*

- Challenge students to find a school-appropriate joke about your lesson topic and then have Open Mic Day.

- Challenge kids to go deeper with humor by including satire or sarcasm in their writing, speeches, artwork, or presentations.

WHAT YOU CAN DO TOMORROW

- **Tell a self-deprecating story.** When I was a ninth-grade Spanish student, a girl passed me a note that said, *Te Amo.* I was a clueless Spaniard, so I blurted out, "What's te amo mean?" I totally screwed up the entire situation, which my students found hilarious.

- **Incorporate a comic.** I've created entire lesson plans based on editorial cartoons.

- **Tell a joke**. If you Google "joke about algebra," or whatever topic you're teaching, you'll strike gold.

- **Display a funny image.** Start the class with an image from your life experience, or from a news story.

- **Begin class with a humorous internet video.** There are countless one-minute videos of dogs doing stupid things. Take just a minute and brighten everyone's day.

- **Challenge students to apply satire or sarcasm to a lesson.** Including humor is so challenging. Your kids will have to understand the topic at a very deep level to be able to pull this off. It'll also be a blast when everyone shares their work.

Invite humor into your classroom and witness profound student enjoyment, which opens the door to greater engagement.

HACK

BRIDGE GENERATION GAPS BY PARLAYING POP CULTURE INTO ENGAGEMENT

THE PROBLEM: TEACHERS OFTEN VIEW POP CULTURE AS A THREAT

IF YOU'VE TAUGHT for any amount of time, you've probably had at least one day where you felt like this gentleman:

> I see no hope for the future of our people if we are dependent on the frivolous youth of today. For certainly all youth are reckless beyond words. When I was a boy, we were taught to be discreet and respectful of elders, but the present generation is exceedingly wise and impatient of restraint.

Ironically, this often-quoted passage, which may be totally apocryphal, is believed to date back to 700 BCE. The source is reported to be Hesiod, the poet of ancient Athens, lamenting two hundred years prior to the Golden Age of Athens. This was a society that was on the way up, yet still, a prominent Athenian felt this way about the city's youth. So your periodic frustration with the world's current crop of kids, your students, is completely understandable and a timeless feature of the human experience.

There's an age gap between my ninth-grade students and me that exceeds forty years. I remember one of my high school teachers who was in his fifties. He seemed like a museum exhibit. I don't want to be like that. Instead, my goal is to be like middle school science teacher Keri Kotchounian and her creative student teacher Brittani Lewis. Keri engages kids by harnessing the power of popular culture.

THE HACK: HARNESS THE POWER OF POP CULTURE

Keri was looking for a new way to teach biomes. She said, "It was closing in on the end of the year, and Brittani and I wanted to keep the kids engaged so we sought out something new and exciting. We found a *Survivor* lesson plan online. We got super excited and started bouncing ideas off one another. We tweaked it and made it our own. One of our primary goals was to hook students immediately. We used Movie Maker and created an awesome opening ceremony video. We took clips from the internet, but then added student names and faces. We also decorated the room. Kids left on Monday and the room looked just like it always did, but then the next morning, there were tiki masks and tropical decorations everywhere.

"The students were intrigued. I could sense them thinking, *What's going on?* But as soon as we mentioned the popular show *Survivor,* they immediately reacted. The kids audibly gasped when we started the video and they saw their faces! They were hooked! When it came to the lesson, the Survivor theme inspired us to create new and engaging activities to inspire students to demonstrate a deep understanding of the elements of a biome, rather than just display them at a more basic level." Obviously, the students were not the only ones engaged and inspired by the Survivor theme.

WHAT YOU CAN DO TOMORROW

- **Research popular shows, songs, and movies.** Discover student listening and watching preferences. You can then conduct internet searches based on these examples.

- **Research classroom applications.** Reality shows are great fodder and many internet search sites will provide great suggestions, if not entire lesson plans.

- **Craft a powerful popular culture hook.** Keri and Brittani decorated their room like a tropical island. They also produced an awesome opening ceremony video.

- **Decorate your room in a theme.** Keri believed decorations served as a strong initial hook and then remained a constant reminder during the duration of the lesson plan.

- **Incorporate traditional classroom learning activities, or come up with new ones.** You don't have to redo your entire lesson from last year to engage students. You can add some elements from pop culture, or do what Keri did and let the spirit move you and revamp or add activities.

Engage students by infusing elements of popular culture into your lesson and your classroom.

HACK

EMPOWER KIDS TO MAKE A 60-SECOND SUPER BOWL COMMERCIAL

THE PROBLEM: TEACHERS NEED TO ADD POW! WHEN TEACHING IMPORTANT CONCEPTS

WINTER IS A rough stretch of highway in Ohio. But the first Sunday in February is a treat. Annually, we host our social circle's Super Bowl party. Our teams from Ohio are never playing in the big game, so it's pretty stress-free. And after we've slurped some full-bodied reds, our gathering becomes more and more focused on the awesome commercials and the over-the-top halftime show. One frigid Super Bowl Sunday, an epic engagement idea struck me like the law of displacement struck Archimedes as he took a bath: *My students need to create Super Bowl commercials.*

THE HACK: CHALLENGE STUDENTS TO MAKE A SUPER BOWL COMMERCIAL

This commercial could obviously be a filmed video, but another option for tech-savvy kids is to challenge them to create an animated commercial on PowToon.

Image 80.1

Image 80.2

PowToon takes chutzpah. There's a bit of a learning curve but it's relatively intuitive with a bit of practice. The primary downside to this platform is that all sound files have to be MP3. Go to the PowToon site via Image 80.1.

Your students may have used PowToon in another class; if not, you'll be amazed at how quickly they learn to manipulate all the awesome tools. I gave them my prompt and I was astounded at how quickly they turned into Madison Avenue advertising gurus! See the commercial I made for my book and podcast by opening the QR code in Image 80.2.

This prompt can be used in any subject at any grade level. Simply make a list of the key vocab terms, events, ideas, and figures from your unit, then assign one to each student. Here's the engaging, challenging, and fun prompt:

- Create a thirty- to sixty-second Super Bowl commercial marketing a concept from the unit. Explain why this concept is important and needs to be included on the assessment.

- Include beautiful images in your commercial.

- The commercial must be uploaded to YouTube. Uploading a video directly from the PowToon platform to YouTube is a breeze.

- Share your video link via your blog.

After all the videos are completed, it's time for the Super Bowl Viewing Party. As classmates watch their peers' commercials, they should record their thoughts about the advertisement and determine whether they think it would be a good test question.

And finally, students can vote on which commercials they like best. There could be various categories like:

- Best Voiceovers

- Best Images

- Best Content

- Most Compelling

WHAT YOU CAN DO TOMORROW

- **Sign up for PowToon.** If you have a Google account, this will take seconds.

- **Create a list of important concepts, events, and individuals.** Consult former unit assessments for ideas.

- **Introduce the prompt with your PowToon creation.** Create your own PowToon ad that describes the prompt, places it in context, and explains why it's important. Going through the process will help you to aid students unfamiliar with PowToon.

- **Show some awesome Super Bowl commercials.** This will stoke creative fires.

- **Create a Google Doc which will help students harvest information.** Students will complete it as they watch classmates' creations.

- **Create a Best Super Bowl Commercial nomination form.** Student nominees will be proud to take a stroll on your classroom's nomination red carpet.

Challenging students to make a Super Bowl commercial for a unit concept is a fun, engaging, and self-directed way for students to learn key concepts in a unit.

HACK

PUSH KIDS UP ON STAGE TO BRING READING ASSIGNMENTS TO LIFE

THE PROBLEM: MANY STUDENTS ARE BORED STIFF BY READING ASSIGNMENTS

I REMEMBER BEING FORCED to read *Great Expectations* in ninth grade. I know – it's a classic work of literature. But for me, at that time in my life, it was pure hell. It seemed totally alien to my existence. It seemed long and exceedingly boring. On a typical day, we'd read silently for about twenty minutes, then we'd answer questions on a worksheet. My friends and I goofed off incessantly during the quiet reading time. I was fourteen and absolutely brimming with testosterone. Sitting still and reading was certainly not my default activity choice. I'm not proud of the way I behaved, but I don't think I got one thing out of that book.

THE HACK: PUSH YOUR STUDENTS UP ON STAGE

I wish I'd had a teacher like Erin Barr. Erin is a middle school intervention specialist. She has a knack for making reading assignments engaging. Even though she focuses on language arts, her methods could be applied to reading in any subject. They could even be used with non-narrative pieces.

She says, "My students have a tough time remembering plot points in stories. They also struggle to grasp advanced concepts. With books or narratives, I challenge students to become characters and act out or create scenes. Assuming a role forces kids to get up and move, which is a great engagement technique. Kids generally insert a lot of humor in their skits. This makes the assignment a lot more enjoyable. After their performances, I'll ask questions like, *Would that character really have been laughing in this scene?* Such questions lead to interesting discussions. Kids, on stage and in the audience, have to put themselves in another's shoes to answer."

Erin also puts a lot of emphasis on nudging her kids to relate the assignment to real life. "As students are planning their skits, I'll ask them, *Have you ever felt that way? Could you show me in the skit?* They'll often recreate a personal experience that's relatable to the reading. Making real-world connections helps everyone understand."

When it comes to a reading assignment, you could assign different groups different segments, or you could ask groups to attack the entire piece but demonstrate different perspectives. You should also be prepared to offer students with stage fright alternatives to performing, such as creating a work of art, a poem, an essay, a podcast, a video, or a blog post.

WHAT YOU CAN DO TOMORROW

- **Create small groups.** These groups will be skit production teams. Arrange students with care and an eye toward productivity.

- **Download a skit outline template.** These are easy to find and will give students direction.

- **Challenge a few groups to make the reading relevant.** They could insert a personal experience, or take a passage from the reading and demonstrate its universal application.

- **Challenge a few groups to pick a boring part of the reading and make it interesting.** See if they can bring an important but dull portion of the reading to life.

- **Challenge a few groups to pantomime what they consider an interesting portion of the reading.** This prompt could be a blast. See if their classmates in the audience can guess what they're depicting.

- **Provide alternatives.** Some kids don't want to act. Give them options.

Many students struggle with sitting and reading. Empower them to get up on stage and show everyone how much they can retain.

HACK

RECITE LAURA'S MANTRA WITH FEELING... *GIVE 'EM VOICE AND GIVE 'EM CHOICE!*

THE PROBLEM: STUDENTS ARE RARELY EMPOWERED TO SAY WHAT THEY WANT, HOW THEY WANT

I THOROUGHLY RESEARCHED ENGAGEMENT for this book. Two themes kept surfacing. I frequently read impassioned pleas for lesson relevance, and I also noticed directives to celebrate and inspire self-directed learning. I'm down with both and try to incorporate each into every lesson. I've learned to do this at the feet of my mentor, the *Voice and Choice Lady,* middle school language arts teacher – Laura Wood. I've learned more from Laura than from any course, administrator, or book.

Relevance and self-directed learning are foundational to student engagement.

THE HACK: FREE KIDS TO MAKE CONNECTIONS AND EXPRESS THEMSELVES

Laura approaches each lesson in the same way. She asks herself these two questions:

1. How can I enable and inspire students to include their voices... as in, what did they get out of the lesson?

2. How can I inspire students to make a choice, as in, how will they express what they've learned?

Laura says, "I once had two students who wanted to show how a character in a story evolved. They approached me with an awesome idea: *We love to bake. We want to show how the character in our assignment changed by baking cupcakes.* Needless to say, I was intrigued." Here's how Laura describes what the students did:

- They filmed themselves at high speed baking cupcakes. When we watched the video, they moved in super-fast-forward. This was cool.

- Their first cupcake attempt was done without a recipe. The girls put what they thought was in cupcakes and just guessed how long they should bake them. They didn't turn out well!

- For the second attempt, they looked at the ingredients…but not the measurements. Again, they turned out poorly, but it was an improvement.

- In the final trial, the girls read the instructions in total, and made great cupcakes.

- The girls concluded their video with a conversation recorded at regular speed. They discussed how the main character in the story we were reading went through a similar self-discovery process. He evolved through trial and error. These girls were totally engaged in demonstrating a deep understanding of the concept. And they demonstrated this understanding doing something they love.

Engage your students with Laura's mantra: *Give 'em Voice and Give 'em Choice.*

WHAT YOU CAN DO TOMORROW

- **Challenge students to list hobbies, passions, interests, and talents.** Encourage kids to write down a number of things. This list will be their *Personal Menu of Demonstration.*

- **Infuse student voice in the lesson.** Ask students to list the major concepts in your current lesson. You may wish to list student answers on your smartboard.

- **Infuse student choice in the lesson.** Prompt students to select a major concept from the lesson and demonstrate it via one of the items on their *Personal Menu of Demonstration*.

- **Schedule a Show-and-Tell Day.** This is where students will unveil their projects to their classmates.

Relevance and self-directed learning are foundational to student engagement. Apply Laura's mantra to each lesson and witness flourishing engagement.

HACK

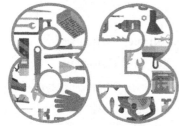

TELEPORT YOUR STUDENTS BACK TO THE 1970S

THE PROBLEM: YOU NEED A FRESH WAY TO GROUP STUDENTS

It's time to offer some pure levity. When students are having fun, they're engaged. Putting students into a group might seem like a mundane task, but it's potentially an outstanding opportunity for teachers to inject some fun.

I went to high school in the 1970s. It was a cosmic time! My peers and I were oddly fascinated with the zodiac. Today, I'll occasionally ask a student, "What's your sign?" and they look at me like I'm nuts. They rarely have a clue what I'm asking. But back in 1977, most kids could tell you their sign, and many could even identify their ideal zodiac match. I'm an Aries, so I had a thing for Leos. Of course, even back in '77, most of us knew that the whole notion of the stars and planets choosing our paths was ridiculous, but nonetheless, it was a fun little diversion. I read my horoscope every day in study hall, and I was not alone in this routine.

THE HACK: GROUP STUDENTS ACCORDING TO ZODIAC COMPATIBILITY

This is an awesome hack if you have a productive class and you're cool with grouping them randomly. Finding information on the zodiac signs is simple. Conduct two searches: The first is a basic description of each sign, and the second is the perfect match for each sign. Once you find fruitful sites, print the information for student handouts. Then comes the fun:

- Make a placard for each zodiac sign, and line up the placards in the hallway about six feet apart. The first placard should be Aries, and the last Pisces.

- Give each student the zodiac information handout. After a minute or two, ask students if their zodiac description is accurate.

- Divide the students into two groups: Alphas and Betas.

- Instruct the Betas to go to the hall and stand on their placard and wait for the Alphas to approach them. This fusses up natural Alphas who are forced to be Betas for this activity.

- Once the Betas have left, hand out the compatibility information to the Alphas. Tell the Alphas to use the table to decide which Betas are their best potential partners. Have them designate a first, second, and third choice.

- Release the Alphas into the hallway. Instruct them that everyone must find a mate based on their first, second, and third choices they created before they saw where the Betas were standing. They must approach then persuade a Beta to partner with them based on the compatibility handout. If they come to an agreement, they shake hands, signal the teacher, and plead their case as to why they have a good partnership. If it's a totally bogus relationship, the teacher should nullify it. The Alpha will have to go in search of new prey, and the Beta will go back to being a wallflower.

- Once everyone has a match, you'll have a line of student pairs stretching down the hallway, and at that point it's simple to divide them into groups.

Ask your students, "Hey…what's your sign?" Good times will be had by all.

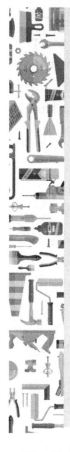

WHAT YOU CAN DO TOMORROW

- **Research zodiac signs.** Create a description handout and a compatibility handout.

- **Create zodiac placards.** Place a placard for each sign in the hallway, about six feet apart.

- **Discuss zodiac descriptions.** Take a little time to talk about the zodiac signs. I like to tell my story about high school. I make it crystal clear to my students that I think the whole notion of the zodiac is silly.

- **Create Alphas and Betas.** You can do this randomly or by temperament. Or, you can fuss up some natural Alphas by making them Betas.

- **Pump up the Alphas.** Send the Betas to the hallway, distribute the compatibility info to the Alphas, challenge them to designate three targets, find their dream partner, and justify it based on zodiac compatibility.

The Zodiac Compatibility Activity will make the mundane task of assigning students to groups a blast! When kids are having fun, they're engaged.

HACK

TRANSFORM TEDIOUS TEST REVIEW

THE PROBLEM: STUDENTS RARELY ENJOY STUDYING

I'M WRITING THIS hack in mid-May. In Central Ohio, schools are closed by Memorial Day. We've got mere days before final exams. The kids look like zombies; the teachers look like zombies; the administrators look even worse. While I'm not a huge fan of final exams, they're part of my school's culture. I'll wager they're part of your school's too. Everyone at my school is getting ready. Students are reviewing, all period, every period. Some are engaged; most aren't. In past years, I've given review sheets and played review games. Those have been moderately effective, but this year, I wanted to try something fun and different. I struck gold with Quizlet. Follow Image 84.1 to the Quizlet homepage.

Image 84.1

THE HACK: USE QUIZLET PRIOR TO YOUR NEXT ASSESSMENT

Quizlet is a cool way to make online flashcards. Students and teachers can sign-in with their Google accounts. I love how Quizlet can be used by kids in solitude, or communally. Students create a stack of flashcards and quiz themselves and classmates. They can do it anywhere and anytime, and they don't have to be near their study partners. I was impressed by how engaged kids were in creating and reviewing their virtual flashcards. They can even add images and voiceovers. Teachers can create study groups and have kids collaborate with Quizlet, and help them discover the fun review games embedded on the site.

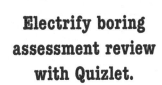

Electrify boring assessment review with Quizlet.

Aside from review activities, Quizlet is also a novel, effective, and engaging way for students to tackle a reading assignment. Instead of a worksheet with questions, or directing kids to highlight and write in the margins, challenge students to create flashcards based on important ideas, figures, and events. They could define, place in context, and determine the significance of each entry. And once again, they can also add cool images and voiceovers. Students can then share their completed sets with you and their classmates in their reading groups. This self-directed approach will be a lot more engaging than answering droning questions on a decade-old worksheet.

WHAT YOU CAN DO TOMORROW

- **Sign in to Quizlet.** If you have a Google account, this takes seconds.

- **Create a silly stack.** Make a few inane flashcards which you can demonstrate to kids.

- **Craft a list of important concepts from your current unit.** You may wish to give students this list, or have them create their own.

- **Challenge students to create their own stacks of virtual flashcards.** The more complete and thorough the list, the better.

- **Designate study groups.** These small groups will collaborate as they study and share virtual flashcards.

- **Consider applying Quizlet to a future reading assignment.** Provide students with an updated way to enhance comprehension.

Electrify boring assessment review with Quizlet.

HACK

TEASE OUT A TASKMASTER WITH GOOGLE CALENDAR

THE PROBLEM: SELF-DIRECTED STUDENTS AREN'T PRODUCTIVE

You've probably experienced this. Your students are navigating a class project. Some kids are on task and rolling. Some kids are totally off-task and meandering. The rest fall somewhere along the productivity spectrum. Here's a dirty little secret about Project Based Learning:

Some students are just not very self-directed when it comes to self-directed learning.

Meandering and unfocused students struggle in the Project Based Learning world. They lack direction. They lack confidence. Be honest, keeping students on task ain't easy.

Ryan Mocarski is a middle school science teacher who has a knack for nudging kids toward productivity, and his class is mostly project based. He says, "I slowly release time-on-task responsibility. For their final project in May, students are 100% self-directed. Between August and May, a bunch of conversations take place between students and me. It's hard for teachers to let students be unproductive. Very early on, I allow this.

This calendar will be their flight plan, their treasure map, their TripTik to productivity.

Then, when they don't complete their projects on time, we have the *What Went Wrong* conversation. Students typically freely admit they didn't use their time well.

"The next step is for me to push those kids to develop a plan of attack for their next project. Over the year, I almost always witness dramatic improvement in productivity and time management. And finally, once students are formulating and executing solid plans, who am I to complain if the kid takes a five-minute break and watches a YouTube video?" I love Ryan's approach. Aim your QR code reader on Image 85.1 to hear Ryan elaborate on his classroom.

Image 85.1

THE HACK: NUDGE YOUR STUDENTS TOWARD PRODUCTIVITY WITH GOOGLE CALENDAR

In order to nurture self-directed learners like Ryan's, it may be necessary to provide students with a planning template. We used to distribute spiral agendas at my school, but the kids wouldn't use them! Well actually, the organized students used them. How's that for irony? A great tool in this important journey of student self-directed productivity is Google Calendar. Google Calendar is totally available to kids who already have Google accounts. If they don't have one, acquiring one takes thirty seconds.

Prompt students to make a twenty-four-hour plan in Google Calendar. They should account for every hour. They should include sleep, watching TV, playing video games, their class schedule, doing homework, basketball practice, eating, and even yakking to their significant other. When completed, direct students to share the calendar. The next day, break students into small groups and prompt them to discuss how successful they were in following their plan. This activity will lay the groundwork for project planning.

Next, direct kids to create a new Google Calendar just for projects. After students designate start and finish dates, they'll fill the void with completion objectives. With a Google Calendar in place, teachers don't have to resort to vague *Let's be more productive* statements. Instead, teachers can meet with students and review how well they've done meeting their Google Calendar objectives.

Google Calendar is a wonderful motivational and accountability tool. So what if a kid takes a five-minute break to text his girlfriend? He's met all his self-imposed objectives for the day! That's engagement.

WHAT YOU CAN DO TOMORROW

- **Create a Google Calendar.** Make a twenty-four-hour plan you can show to students as a model.

- **Direct students to create a Google Calendar.** Many might already have one.

- **Challenge students to make their own twenty-four-hour plan.** This activity will lead to some fascinating evaluation conversations in small groups the next day.

- **Prompt students to create a new Google Project Calendar.** This calendar will be their flight plan, their treasure map, their TripTik to productivity.

Google Calendar is a great productivity and motivational tool for self-directed learners.

HACK

ENCOURAGE STUDENTS TO SNEAK OUT OF YOUR ROOM

THE PROBLEM: ASSESSMENTS NEED MORE COLLABORATION, CREATIVITY, AND MOVEMENT

Jennifer Zimmer teaches high school Spanish. Her students were working toward a unit assessment, and she longed to do something new. Jennifer decided to approach Kristen Macklin, her District Media Specialist, and Jason Manly, the District Instructional Facilitator. Great decision! Kristen and Jason hatched the idea of an escape room. This lesson plan was a major success and inspired new roles for Kristen and Jason. Their school now has the luxury of housing two Escape Room Architects-in-Residence. Their initial creation, which I'll highlight in this hack, coaxed student problem-solving, collaboration, and creative thinking skills all while students communicated with one another in Spanish.

THE HACK: INTRODUCE MOVEMENT, ENGAGEMENT, AND FUN TO YOUR NEXT UNIT WITH AN ESCAPE ROOM

When I asked Kristen where she got the idea for student escape rooms, she answered quickly: "Our principal went to one with his kids and loved it. Then, Jennifer Zimmer appeared and asked for an assessment idea. I did a little research, found an article about educational escape rooms, and then approached Jason Manly with the concept." As I listened to Kristen, I recalled a *Big Bang Theory* episode where Amy, Emily, Leonard, and Raj visit an escape room. Being the brilliant characters they are, they burned through the clues quickly and escaped. Nonetheless, the room itself was cool, the props were compelling, and the puzzles they solved would be quite challenging for the typical student.

Creating such a learning experience may seem like a tall order. Jason suggests that intrigued teachers visit breakoutedu.com for ideas, explanations, examples, and an online store to purchase equipment. Image 86.1 will take you to the site.

Kristen has inventoried many props that make escape rooms possible. She and Jason use combination locks, QR codes, jigsaw puzzles, hollowed-out books, toolkits, tackle boxes, lock boxes, and bicycle chains with locks – and their collection keeps expanding.

Jason suggests that teachers place a lot of effort on creating engaging and challenging prompts. Then architects like him and Kristen can build exciting escape room puzzles from

Image 86.1

these teacher-generated prompts. The student objective is simple: Small groups must solve a puzzle to get directions to the next puzzle. The ultimate objective is to be freed from the room. This occurs only after mastering many obstacles.

Jennifer Zimmer's students were required to navigate the escape room conversing only in Spanish. "This experience gave students the freedom to use Spanish in a real-world situation. Students were not obsessing over how to say something like they would on a test, but just communicating conversationally as effectively as possible."

As students worked feverishly to escape, Jennifer cruised around the room, assessing their conversations. Her students gave this experience glowing reviews. She heard, "I didn't feel like I was taking a test! We were just having fun using the language." Open the link in Image 86.2 to hear science teacher Kayla DeMuth discuss an escape room. You can also access the contact information for Kristen Macklin and Jason Manly.

Image 86.2

WHAT YOU CAN DO TOMORROW

- **Research educational escape rooms**. You'll find plenty of examples and instructions with a basic Google search.
- **Share a Google Form with colleagues.** See if you can find some like-minded colleagues who'd like to explore this concept.

Jennifer Zimmer would've been lost without the help of Kristen and Jason. Finding like-minded colleagues could also help in terms of gathering props and the creation process.

- **Approach administrators.** Hopefully, they'll be on board with the idea. They may even be willing to pitch in some financial resources to prop acquisition. They also may have suggestions on where the escape room could be located. Perhaps there's an available room in the building.

- **Create engaging and challenging puzzles.** This is entirely your job. In the *Big Bang Theory* episode, the characters solved the puzzles too quickly. It's better to make them too challenging than too easy.

For your next assessment, challenge your students to escape. Ironically, they may not want to leave because they're having too much fun.

HACK

BE OBSERVANT AND FIND THE ELUSIVE SPARK

THE PROBLEM: TEACHERS DON'T KNOW THEIR STUDENTS

TEACHERS OFTEN GET swept up in student achievement. That's totally understandable. It's one of our primary jobs. But teachers also have an obligation to foster student passion. When students pursue their passion, their spark – they're engaged. That spark is hidden in some students. Some students aren't even aware of their own passions. You can help.

THE HACK: SEARCH FOR THE SPARK IN EACH STUDENT

Become an undercover investigator early in the semester. Assign various types of hands-on activities which free you to cruise around and ask all sorts of questions: some pertaining to the activity, others to learn about student interests, and some to help you get to know kids better. Here are some examples:

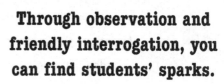

Through observation and friendly interrogation, you can find students' sparks.

- How do you like this activity?

- What's your favorite class?

- Who's your favorite teacher?

- What would you rather be doing?

- What do you like to do on the weekend?

- What's the first thing you do when you get home from school?

- What do you do well?

- How would you improve this assignment?

- How could we expand this assignment?

In addition to asking questions:

- Keenly observe them working.

- Listen to what they say to one another.

- Evaluate their products.

As soon as you see or sense that little spark, try to confirm it. "You seem to enjoy watching YouTube. For our next unit, would you like to create a documentary about the Arab-Israeli Conflict and then post it online?" It will be evident immediately if you struck gold. If not, keep searching for the spark. The potential payoffs are huge. Through observation and friendly interrogation, you can find students' sparks. Kids are intensely engaged when they pursue their passions.

WHAT YOU CAN DO TOMORROW

- **Create an activity where students have many options of expression.** Allow students to choose their methods for expression. This will be an excellent first step in finding their sparks.

- **Promote an example.** Frequently tell stories of past students who thrived once they started chasing their passions.

- **Become a private investigator.** The subtle nature of your investigation is important in finding the spark. Students don't like being involuntary lab rats. Just observe and question in a friendly, casual way.

- **Exploit what you learn.** Once you discover the sparks, they will shape how you motivate and interact with students.

Finding a student's spark and then exploiting that spark is a key to engagement. Teachers can find this spark through observation and interaction.

HACK

ISSUE THE 1,000 PUSHUP CHALLENGE

THE PROBLEM: YOU NEED TO BECOME MORE APPROACHABLE

MY BOOK, *You've Gotta Connect*, which gives teachers tools to forge strong relationships with students, was published in 2014. In this work, I promote the essential nature of teacher approachability. We sometimes forget that kids may find us distant, intimidating, or both. The forging of strong student-teacher relationships is often the prerequisite to deep engagement. In order to foster these bonds, teachers must be approachable and then become familiar. One ultra enjoyable way to encourage positive student-teacher relationships is to issue a self-improvement challenge. In this hack, I'll model a physical challenge. That may not attract you or a portion of your kids, but consider this hack a template. I'll provide some non-athletic challenges later in the hack. In the meantime, ladies and gentleman, start your metabolisms.

THE HACK: CHALLENGE KIDS TO DO 1,000 PUSHUPS

On a raw December Ohio morning during my commute to school, I came up with the harebrained scheme of pulling my students into one of my ridiculous weekend body-weight workout challenges. I'm still a fit guy and my students admire that. I occasionally talk about my diverse workout routines, and such monologues often lead to students sharing some of their favorite workouts. I decided to promote the idea of students joining me in my objective of completing 1,000 pushups on a Saturday. I just casually floated the objective and was impressed by the student response. Half of my kids enthusiastically wanted to join me.

The challenge was engaging in itself, but we decided to add more intense peer pressure. We created a Voxer 1,000 Pushups Group. This inspired intense competition. Participants let others know exactly where they were on the road to 1,000. Some students would just record their voices: *I just hit 600, only 400 to go!* Other brave souls upped their game by adding video and images of themselves executing pushup after pushup. Some ostentatious teachers did the same. Any guess as to whom? A wonderful dividend of migrating the challenge to Voxer was that many non-participants became engaged spectators. One could join the Voxer group whether one was a participant or not.

Interestingly enough, the female participation in the pushup challenge was not what I wanted. So the next weekend, my class engaged in the 1,000 Squat Challenge. My young women literally stepped up and laid waste to patriarchy. Two days after the challenge, on a frigid, dark, early winter Monday morning, students were chirping away about their Saturday squatting spree. Who knew soreness could be so engaging?

Please rest assured that you don't have to be a jock to issue a challenge to students. Try these ideas on for size:

- How many pages can you read on a Saturday?

- How early can you wake up on a Saturday?

- How nice can you be to your family on a Saturday?

- How many family members can you feed on a Saturday?

- How charitable can you be on a Saturday?

- How many hours can you go without your phone on a Saturday?

And, if you have a hard time coming up with a challenge, ask your kids. They'll probably come up with something even better. Please follow the QR code in Image 88.1 to hear my students discuss their experiences in the 1,000 Pushup Challenge.

Image 88.1

WHAT YOU CAN DO TOMORROW

- **Concoct a weekend challenge that will inspire a majority of your kids.** Please check out some of my suggestions, or prompt students to come up with one. It does not have to be linked to your curriculum. Mine certainly wasn't!

- **Designate a day.** Saturdays are great because many kids are home and have fewer obligations.

- **Determine which social media you'll use to keep track of progress.** Voxer is perfect for this challenge because kids can so readily check in on one another once they join the group you create for this eventful Saturday.

This bonding activity will not take one moment away from instruction. Forge relationships, inject fun, and watch joyously as those stronger relationships translate to student growth.

HACK

REBOOT WITH KAHOOT!

THE PROBLEM: MOST LESSON ASSESSMENTS ARE STALE REVIEWS

AFTER I'VE TAUGHT a lesson for a few years, I get comfortable with it. I internalize the material. I learn what techniques and activities engage students. But I have to confess, I can get a little too comfortable. One key way I maintain my edge is to try new things, and that's exactly why I decided to try Kahoot!.

I saw Kahoot! demonstrated at an inservice, and I thought, *That looks cool. Maybe I'll try Kahoot! someday.* I also was intrigued because the presenter kept saying how much kids love it. I remember thinking, O*kay, my seventh-grade English teacher raved about how much we would love diagramming sentences. That was false advertising.* I decided to see if the Kahoot! presenter was selling me a bill of goods.

THE HACK: USE KAHOOT! AS A FORMATIVE ASSESSMENT

My students recently completed a lesson on ISIS, so I decided to take Kahoot! on a test drive. I typed ten multiple-choice review questions. Below is an example of an old-school question delivery method:

Which of the following does NOT represent a way in which ISIS gets its money?

A. Military aid from Iran

B. Oil revenues

C. Ransom for hostages

D. Donations from sympathetic individuals around the world

(The answer is A...if you're curious.)

In the olden days, I would've duplicated a paper copy of my ten questions and distributed one to each student. Or, I'd have announced the questions and directed kids to record their answers. Now, I'd be more inclined to create a Google Form, but even that gets stale. I wanted to try something new.

I created a Kahoot! quiz by simply copying and pasting my questions and answers into the Kahoot! template. It was remarkably easy. See my Kahoot! quiz in Image 89.1.

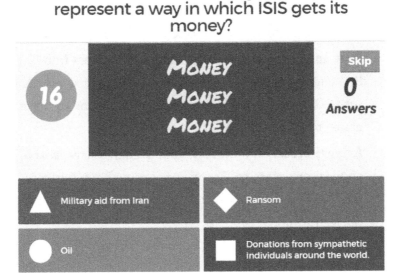

Image 89.1

Students won't have to create a username and password. They'll simply go to Kahoot.it and enter a six-digit game pin that you provide. The simplicity of Kahoot! is a major plus.

On my Kahoot! maiden voyage, I instructed students to take out their devices, be it phone or Chromebook. A couple of students had neither, so I allowed them to pair up with someone who did (you can use Kahoot! in team mode in case there aren't enough devices). I was amazed by how easily students picked up on Kahoot!. I displayed questions on the smartboard and they responded on their devices. Kahoot! indicated the correct answer and the *Top 3 Leader Board* after each round. Points are awarded based on speed and accuracy. It's a wonderful way to engage students in a review. My kids love to compete and when the correct answer and winning scores were revealed, their reactions were quite animated.

That young man who exposed me to Kahoot! and promised student enthusiasm was totally on-point.

WHAT YOU CAN DO TOMORROW

- **Write ten review questions.** Take tomorrow's lesson and craft ten multiple-choice questions.

- **Create a Kahoot! account.** Follow the QR code I provided earlier or go to www.kahoot.com.

- **Copy and paste your ten questions and answers into Kahoot!.** Remember, students compete not only on accuracy, but also speed. You may wish to adjust some questions to make them easier to digest rapidly.

- **Arrange students.** If most of your students have smartphones, or access to Chromebooks, you're in business. If not, see if you can pair students who don't have devices with those who do.

Kahoot! is a magnificent way to engage students in lesson review.

HACK

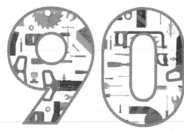

ENROLL YOUR STUDENTS IN PHOTOJOURNALISM

THE PROBLEM: IMAGES ARE UNDERUSED IN THE CLASSROOM

CERTAINLY, YOU'VE HEARD the old cliché: *A picture is worth a thousand words.* I did some research on this statement and was delighted to learn that prior to photography, individuals used to say: *A painting is worth a thousand words.* Images, whether captured or manufactured, are powerful. I cannot remember the last tweet I sent that was imageless. Social media is fueled by compelling images. We need to capitalize on this natural human attraction.

Using images properly is an essential practice for kids to internalize.

THE HACK: TRANSFORM YOUR STUDENTS INTO PHOTOJOURNALISTS

Here are five iconic images from American history:

- The painting of George Washington crossing the Delaware.

- The WWI Uncle Sam recruiting poster.

- The Marines hoisting the flag on Iwo Jima.

- Lyndon Johnson taking the oath of office beside a stunned and blood-stained Jackie Kennedy.

- Associates of Dr. King standing over his body, pointing toward an assassin.

Do any of these descriptions conjure up mental images? Do they inspire emotions, or perhaps personal narratives? If you weren't familiar with some of these images, did you Google the description out of curiosity?

I was recently teaching about the Rape of Nanking. This pivotal Chinese city was brutalized by the invading Japanese in 1937, and yet Americans are largely ignorant of this atrocity. The Japanese so abused the residents of Nanking, that even Nazi diplomats stationed in the city were horrified. I needed more than just my words, or a narrative, to tell this story, so I opened my lesson with horrifying images. The following Google Slides were presented through Pear Deck. Please follow this QR code in Image 90.1 to access my presentation, but be advised, the images are graphic.

My students were intensely engaged after this presentation. I prompted them frequently on Pear Deck throughout my presentation. I invited them to collaborate with their peers. Once I concluded, they were desperate to learn how

Image 90.1

such an atrocity could have happened. None of this curiosity would have been present if it weren't for those disturbing images.

Challenge your students to become photojournalists and tell a story with images. You could prompt them to create a Google Slides presentation like mine. The great thing about creating such a presentation is the image search feature in Google. It automatically finds usage-appropriate images for students. Using images properly is an essential practice for kids to internalize. Another option is for students to create their own images. Last semester, we navigated a blog prompt on Chinese landscape art. Students were encouraged to capture a landscape. Most snapped a photo with their phones, but a few brave souls actually drew their submissions. A very cool app that you can use to make a photo appear like an amazing painting is Prisma. Many of my students took an image on their phones and morphed it with this app. Open Image 90.2 to visit my blog prompt, which gives an example and instructions on how one can access Prisma, and beautiful examples of what can be done with a simple picture.

Image 90.2

Image 90.3

Follow the QR code in Image 90.3 to hear one of my students explain how images can be impactful in the classroom.

WHAT YOU CAN DO TOMORROW

- **Create a Google Slide presentation with compelling images about tomorrow's lesson.** These images should be accompanied by sparse text...no more than just a title on each slide.

- **Present with Pear Deck.** Load your Google Slides into Pear Deck so you can prompt students as you travel through the presentation.

- **Challenge students to create their own Google Slides presentations based on your template.** Like your presentation, theirs should be image-rich and text-poor.

- **Create a prompt where students must create their own images.** Consider incorporating the Prisma app to make their images awesome.

A picture is worth a thousand words, so save your breath and liberate their imaginations!

HACK

REVOLUTIONIZE THE FIELD TRIP

THE PROBLEM: STUDENTS DON'T GET OUT MUCH

I WENT TO ELEMENTARY school a long time ago. Amazingly, some of my most vivid school memories are of the field trips we took, and we took a lot of them. I grew up in the small town of New Concord, Ohio. It's a beautiful little college town nestled in the hills of the Southeastern part of the Buckeye State. For field trips, we went to the bank, the post office, the glass blower, and the dairy, but my favorite excursion was to the bakery. A half-century later, those experiences are still etched in my memory. I must have been pretty darned engaged in learning how to make a doughnut! Don't you remember almost everything about your middle school trip to Washington, D.C.?

THE HACK: GUIDE STUDENTS ON A VIRTUAL TOUR WITH CHUTZPAH

When I was a student, you had to go to such places as a museum, dairy, or pottery studio to experience learning outside the classroom. Budgets, legal reasons, and downright fussiness prevent many field trips in contemporary education. In the true spirit of Hacking Engagement, it's time to devise a way to bring back the field trip and create memories that will last deep into the 21st century.

The internet frees learners to take virtual tours anytime, anywhere, and there is no admission fee. In my World Civ class, we worked our way through a lesson on the earliest forms of art. The artwork on the cave walls of Lascaux in Southern France could be some of the world's oldest. The spectacular paintings of gazelles, bison, horses, and more than 900 other animals date back eighteen thousand years. How in the world would prehistoric man have had the time, the inclination, and the aptitude to create those wondrous images? That's precisely the kind of question that drives engaging and impactful learning! While it would be breathtaking to visit the caves, students can take an awesome virtual tour of Southern France by opening this QR code (Image 91.1).

Image 91.1

Image 91.2

If you're wondering if such a trip might only work in the humanities, you're thinking too small. *Education Week* contributor Liana Heitin featured Marva Hinton's blog post "How Virtual Field Trips Can Change Science Class" in a 2016 article. Read the article in Image 91.2.

WHAT YOU CAN DO TOMORROW

- **Deputize travel consultants.** Search the internet for interesting virtual travel experiences that relate to your lesson. Better yet – let your students find a cool virtual tour, for even more engagement potential. Kids are good at finding resources! This destination selection experience is a lot like being a parent. You want to go hiking in Colorado, but your kids want to go to Myrtle Beach. Guess where you'll end up?

- **Conduct a *Your Mission* briefing.** In WWII movies, a typical scene is of American pilots opening up their attack target envelopes in the tense mission briefing prior to their flights. If your students found a number of cool virtual tours, break

them into small groups and assign different targets to different groups. You may wish to put the mission objectives and the essential questions into envelopes for them to tear open.

- **Invite virtual chaperones.** We always had moms accompany us on our elementary field trips. They were there to help corral us. That's not necessary with a virtual field trip, but inviting chaperones would still be really cool. Let parents see what you're doing in class. Students will love their presence.

- **Blog about the experience**. A great way for learners to respond to essential questions about a virtual tour is to respond virtually. They could type a post, create a video or a short podcast, forge an artifact, post pictures, and describe it. Or, they could come up with a novel way to express themselves.

Field trips are quite engaging. Ignore the logistical nightmare of the modern field trip and take frequent and impactful virtual excursions.

═ HACK ═

BUILD YOUR OWN SMITHSONIAN

THE PROBLEM: TAKING YOUR STUDENTS TO THE SMITHSONIAN IS IMPRACTICAL

I DID NOT VISIT the National Air and Space Museum till I was in my twenties. I was inspired because I had just read Tom Wolfe's book, *The Right Stuff,* which was about post-WWII test pilots and the original Mercury astronauts. I was visiting my sister, who lived in Arlington, Virginia. I decided to go downtown and see some awesome chariots of the sky in person. I entered this hallowed building, rounded a corner, and was greeted by the beautiful orange and diminutive *X-1*, Chuck Yeager's plane that broke the sound barrier in 1947. On this magical afternoon, I also stood mere feet from the *Friendship 7*, John Glenn's tiny capsule dented from debris during his perilous re-entry into our atmosphere. John Glenn is from my hometown of New Concord, Ohio, and I graduated from John Glenn High School. And finally, I gazed up and saw the elegant, shiny, silver, canvas-covered *Spirit of St. Louis*, which Charles Lindbergh flew across the Atlantic in 1927.

I felt like a boy. I was in wonder. The fascinating books I'd read, the engaging stories I'd heard, all materialized on that muggy Washington afternoon. I want you to create this powerful sense of wonder in your classroom.

THE HACK: COMMISSION STUDENTS TO CREATE THEIR OWN SMITHSONIAN

Your first task is logistical. You must decide where in your building your Smithsonian will materialize. Your classroom is too small. Opt for the gymnasium, the cafeteria, or the atrium. If the weather cooperates and your Wi-Fi is sufficient, outdoors may also be an option. Your next task is to sort your students by roles:

- Physical curators build and then present artifacts.

- Virtual curators build and then present virtual exhibits and display them on Chromebooks.

- Dramatic curators assume the role and identity of characters. They are their own exhibits!

- Researchers are students who prefer to work behind the scenes and are on call to help curators with exhibit creation.

- Museum promoters advertise your Smithsonian on social media.

- Salespeople cold-call potential clients and create and distribute admission coupons, which they must collect on opening day.

Challenge students to bring the unit you're studying to life! If you're studying Imperialism, your museum could be called *The National Smithsonian Imperialism Museum*. With six potential roles to select from and wide-open exhibit potential, student engagement should flourish. For curators and researchers, there are plenty of online resources devoted to creating virtual museum exhibits and living wax museums. The promotion types will have a lot of fun in their realm. They must first name the museum, then they can promote their creation on your class website, school website, Google Classroom, and Twitter. A great place for salespeople to find potential attendees is study hall. If your class meets third period, direct some top-notch pitch-people to the study hall teacher. It's been my experience that study hall monitors are totally down with you stealing a healthy number of their students. Other potential guests include administrators both at the building and district levels, teachers who have conference periods, and parents! Salespeople should also be in charge of customer satisfaction surveys. They'll obtain valuable feedback for exhibitors.

WHAT YOU CAN DO TOMORROW

- **Scout your school.** You want a large open space so guests can walk around. You also don't want curator voices competing, so it's good to have physical distance between exhibits.

- **Sort students.** Advertise each of the six roles. This is a project where students can work independently or with classmates. Students like this option!

- **Brainstorm ideas.** Have students call out important concepts from the unit. Write these ideas on the smartboard. These will help curators come up with ideas for exhibits.

- **Meet with curators and researchers.** Have each present their exhibit idea for approval. Brainstorm ways to use researchers.

- **Meet with promoters and sales staff.** Direct them to present their plans for approval. Make suggestions and be sure to review their customer satisfaction surveys in advance.

Self-directed learning and creating opportunities for kids to do what they enjoy are crucial ingredients for student engagement. Both will be included when your class creates its own Smithsonian.

HACK

APPLY TONI'S TEMPLATE FOR ENGAGING RELUCTANT LEARNERS

THE PROBLEM: IT'S HARD TO ENGAGE RELUCTANT LEARNERS

D ID YOU...

- Graduate from high school with at least a 3.00 GPA?

- Play a varsity sport?

- Become a member of the National Honor Society?

Teachers who were academically successful participated in sports, were members of extracurricular groups, and experience warm feelings when they think about their school days (this describes a lot of educators). They are also at a significant disadvantage when it comes to understanding the perspectives of reluctant learners. It's also possible they have a hard time relating to minority students who may feel alienated because of race, ethnicity, or sexual identity.

It's your responsibility to forge a relationship.

A teacher's gender can be a titanic barrier as well. I've always been intrigued by how some female instructors are champs at engaging reluctant male students, while other female teachers struggle mightily with such kids. I decided to consult an expert, a champion, a guru – and find out how she does it.

THE HACK: TONI'S TEMPLATE

Toni Newton has lived in Cleveland her whole life. She started teaching in Cleveland Public and then migrated to the inner-ring district of South Euclid. She recently intervened in a confrontation. She says, "A young male student kept mumbling his name and refusing to take out his earbuds when questioned by a female staff member. She became very upset and started yelling. He responded by clenching his fists. His body began shaking. He was barely able to contain himself. I know this kid and realized that I better jump in. I took him aside and just started talking. Not lecturing…just distracting him, hoping to cool him down. I nodded to my colleague as if to say, *I got this*. Unfortunately, she didn't take the hint. On two different occasions, I calmed him down only to have her circle back and continue her lecture! She kept escalating the situation. This young African-American male was being totally backed into a corner. She had no appreciation of his perspective. All she cared about was getting the last word."

When it comes to mentoring young colleagues struggling to engage reluctant male students, Toni advises:

- Be patient. Bonding with reluctant learners takes time.

- Don't take things personally. Kids can treat you miserably, but be the adult and don't take the bait.

- Let them get to know you. Toni once helped a young white teacher who was struggling to engage his African-American students. She encouraged him to share his love of heavy metal music. Remarkably, and after some failed attempts, it worked.

- Be authentic. Reluctant learners love to find your weaknesses. Don't try to be something you're not.

WHAT YOU CAN DO TOMORROW

- **Highlight students on your roster.** As I go down through my current crop of kids, it's easy for me to highlight students who process the world differently than me.

- **Compose a brief perspective description for each highlighted student.** These are one- or two-sentence reflections such as, *Jason seems very religious*, or *Niki is very vocal about her democratic views*. Some may be disturbing, such as, *Hans seems inclined toward white supremacy*. Such reflections will help you

navigate future student interactions. Regardless of whether you agree with your students, it's your responsibility to forge a relationship.

- **Break down barriers by sharing a hobby.** Toni's students from Cleveland Public probably didn't listen to a lot of heavy metal, but nonetheless, her young colleague took her advice and engaged his students. What interesting hobbies could you share that might particularly interest young males?

Many teachers struggle to understand the perspective of reluctant learners. Engage such kids by patiently applying Toni's template.

HACK

PRESCRIBE ART AS AN ANTIDOTE FOR ASSESSMENT ANXIETY

THE PROBLEM: MANY STUDENTS FREEZE WHEN CONFRONTED WITH AN ESSAY ASSESSMENT PROMPT

NOAH HEATH IS young, high-tech, popular, and unorthodox psychology teacher. He pushes envelopes. He questions standard operating procedures. Just my kind of guy. I recently walked into his room and noticed some interesting artwork on the wall. I asked about it. The next ten minutes simply evaporated as Noah described his recent assessment experiment. He said, "I have a lot of students who are uncomfortable with traditional tests. I wanted to give these kids an option. I let them opt to use art to demonstrate mastery of altered states of consciousness. They were to compare chemically altered consciousness (through drugs) and non-chemically altered consciousness (through hypnosis, meditation, and biofeedback). Traditionally, I give students an essay asking them to compare and contrast. Students who participated in my experiment still had to include a writing component, but it was to explain their artwork. Their creation did the job of comparing and contrasting."

THE HACK: EMPOWER STUDENTS TO DEMONSTRATE LEARNING THROUGH AN ART PROJECT

Select an essay prompt from your next assessment. Give students the option of demonstrating their learning with an art project. Noah gave kids simple instructions that sponsored incredible expression. "They were allowed to use any medium and to create whatever they wanted, but their work had to demonstrate comparing and contrasting of altered states in a deep way. They also had to thoroughly explain their artifact and how it addressed the prompt. I was amazed by the number of takers. Apparently, a lot of students don't like essays." See a student's art project in Image 94.1.

Image 94.1

Noah's students were extremely engaged in their projects. It's challenging to explain a complex concept like altered consciousness with art. Students had

Image 94.2

to focus, experiment, take risks, consult with peers, revise, and at times – start over. After students completed their masterpieces, they had to explain them. Noah believes the entire enterprise fostered a far deeper understanding than merely studying and then taking a traditional assessment. Open the QR code in Image 94.2 to listen to Noah elaborate on this hack.

WHAT YOU CAN DO TOMORROW

- **Create an art-worthy prompt.** For ideas, list some key learning objectives in the unit you're studying. Review extended response questions you've used previously. Compare-and-contrast questions work well.

- **Expose students to a famous work of art and enlighten them about its deep meaning.** An excellent example is Pablo Picasso's *Guernica*, which was painted during the Spanish Civil War.

- **Challenge students to brainstorm ways to demonstrate learning other than essay writing.** List the examples they come up with on the board. Interesting ideas may include graffiti, poetry, sculpture, music, or photography.

- **Call for student proposals.** Indicate that before kids can embark on their artistic assessment journey, they must clear their flight plan with you.

Many students suffer with traditional assessments. Experiment with allowing them to demonstrate deep understanding with art.

HACK

HARNESS PASSIONS TO ENGAGE STUDENT NETWORKING

THE PROBLEM: NETWORKING IS AN ESSENTIAL SKILL THAT'S RARELY TAUGHT

I ABSOLUTELY HATE WHAT I'm going to write in this paragraph, but it's brutally honest. I teach Social Studies. I've taught at three different high schools. In each case, I would never have been interviewed if I hadn't coached football. When I think of all the amazing teachers who never get opportunities because they don't coach a sport, it makes me sad! I didn't create this phenomenon, but I had to work within it. My goal was to network to get an interview. Then, I believed, I'd have a fair shot at getting the job.

My plan worked. My initial objective was to meet the head football coach. If I made a favorable impression on him, I hoped he would be willing to pass my name along to the principal. I went three for three with this approach. I never knew the coach before asking for a meeting. I just boldly went where no James Sturtevant had gone before! I told these gentlemen that I could help their football program and would love the opportunity to teach at their school. I then asked if they'd be willing to mention me to their principals.

THE HACK: INSPIRE STUDENTS TO NETWORK

Networking is an important skill, but it's also an inclination. Some people really struggle to put themselves out there. It could be shyness, or a feeling that networking is shamelessly self-promotional. This hack will help learners overcome these hurdles.

I've had kids work on career paths, set goals, and create future plans, but often these activities felt abstract. When you're sixteen, describing your life ten years into the future is more than half a lifetime fast-forward. Instead, inspire students to network about something they're passionate about right now. Have them network about their hobbies. While writing this manuscript, I became obsessed with creating my *Hacking Engagement Podcast*. It was a blast learning how to produce, design, and perform on the show. It's my hobby and I love talking about it. When I have questions about podcasting and my research is not yielding answers, I network! Some cool relationships have emerged as a result.

Challenge your students to proclaim their hobbies. It could be anything school-appropriate:

- Skateboarding

- Weightlifting

- Cooking

- Surfing

- Boxing

- Anime

- Role-play

Then, ask them to create at least five questions they have about their passions. The questions could be anything technical, such as:

While lifting weights, what's better: high weight and low reps, or low weight and high reps?

Or, they could be something big-picture:

What are some trending jobs in the culinary field?

These questions must be authentic; things that students wonder about.

Challenge learners to go on an expert hunt. They can search Amazon for successful authors. They can find a popular blog about any school-appropriate hobby. Blogs are a great option because bloggers generally respond to comments. Guide students to craft a friendly plea to answer their burning hobby questions. Make certain they also ask if there's another person they should try to contact. This activity will really engage your students.

Finally, students must complete and submit a Google Form recounting their networking experience. This will be your electronic accountability paper trail. Here are some prompt suggestions:

- Attach a screenshot of your conversation thread with your hobby expert.

- Was this interaction helpful?

- Did this interaction inspire you to contact anyone else? If so, elaborate!

- In the next twenty-four hours, network about something else. It must be something you want, but need help getting. Describe your experience below.

- Describe how networking could help you in the future.

See a sample of the Networking Debriefing Form in Image 95.1.

Networking Debriefing

* Required

Add a screenshot of your conversation thread with your hobby expert. *

Your answer

Was this interaction helpful? *

Your answer

Did this interaction inspire you to contact anyone else? If so...elaborate! *

Your answer

In the next 24 hours, network about something else. It must be something you want, but need help getting. Describe your experience below. *

Your answer

Describe how networking could help you in the future. *

Your answer

Image 95.1: Google and the Google logo are registered trademarks of Google Inc., used with permission.

Once learners get more engaged with networking, just imagine what they could discover about your next lesson.

WHAT YOU CAN DO TOMORROW

- **Talk about the power of networking.** I recounted my story about getting my teaching positions. If you have a job, you probably have a networking story to share, too.

- **Challenge students to select a hobby.** Some kids might be a little coy on this front, but keep persuading. Direct them to list more than one if they're willing, but implore them to choose something that makes them passionate.

- **Challenge students to email experts.** They can search authors on Amazon and also popular blogs. Once they find their experts, kids need to contact them and ask them questions.

- **Debrief students.** A great way to do this is through a Google Form. It can also be done with paper and pencil.

Engage students by inspiring them to explore their hobbies, while simultaneously learning about the power and potential of networking.

HACK

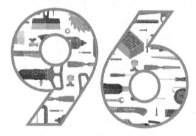

RESCUE KIDS FROM THE ACADEMIC ASSEMBLY LINE

THE PROBLEM: RIGID TEMPLATES STIFLE STUDENTS

IF YOU THINK about the typical student day, it seems kids proceed down a massive assembly line. From the moment they walk in the door, they are funneled into crowded hallways, and required to jam their stuff into rows of standardized lockers. Inspired by the gong of a bell, they march to identical-looking rooms, are nourished at noon with cloned meals on standard-issue plastic trays with indented compartments, and finally are ushered out of the building at exactly the same time. It's perfectly rational to expect that what is produced during this highly structured day at the factory would be remarkably uniform. I'm surprised kids haven't unionized.

Teaching will now mean meandering around the room inspiring, brainstorming, evaluating, and bonding.

The ubiquitous writing template is a micro-example of this factory mindset. I have to confess, I love it when I'm supplied with a writing template. My publisher imposed a template on me for this book, and I'd be lost without it. While templates provide direction and form, they're incredibly restrictive. They don't encourage creativity, individuality, or innovation. Unfettered expression and relevance are primary ingredients in engagement. Templates have their place, but frequently, kids need to be rescued.

THE HACK: EXPERIMENT BY BAGGING A HIGHLY STRUCTURED WRITING PROMPT

Students generally don't write well and many don't enjoy doing it. The template mentality doesn't help with toning those creative muscles or with the fun factor. Consequently, teachers shy away from assigning much writing. However, the only way our students will get better at this essential skill is practice. Writing prompts should be included, regardless of the subject. Yes, even math teachers should encourage kids to write. These writing excursions don't need to be long research papers. Students can write sentences and paragraphs and then do a peer review. The process doesn't need to be formal. The key is to get kids expressing themselves through writing.

I'm passionate in this area because I was a reluctant writer. Magically, I evolved into a confident writer once my words started to match my speech. I remember joyfully thinking as I proofed a paper in college, *Wow! This is the first time I've written something that actually sounds like me.* I evolved to the blessed stage of confidence by navigating unstructured writing prompts. My classmates and I were challenged to simply express ourselves in short literary bursts. Often, kids whine that they don't know what to write. I know I did. However, kids whine about a lot of things that are good for them and often those bellows reflect simple insecurity. Be patient with this process and encourage your students to do the same.

My kids do a fair amount of writing in my dual-credit history class. I love the organization of the five-paragraph essay. This template gives students a tool to demonstrate their understanding. However, this tool often leads to the mass production of student essays that read remarkably the same. There is certainly a place for this mode of instruction, but perhaps it's overdone.

How about doing a little experiment? Select a learning outcome from the unit you're teaching. Perhaps you have a worn lesson matched with this outcome that needs a fresh coat of paint. Provide students with the following:

- The learning outcome

- A simple writing prompt, such as: *How would you teach this concept to someone outside of our class?*

- A basic rubric

- A deadline

Teaching will now mean meandering around the room inspiring, brainstorming, evaluating, and bonding. Students may initially struggle with this freedom. A few will continue to struggle, but many will blossom. Issuing this open-ended prompt will take courage on your part but could lead to massive intellectual growth in your students.

WHAT YOU CAN DO TOMORROW

- **Create a sparse prompt.** If you're studying nutrition, challenge them, "Today, students, I want you to write about nutrition."

- **Indicate a length objective.** "How much do we have to write?" This question will materialize quickly, particularly if kids aren't accustomed to unstructured prompts. You could tell them to write two fantastic complete sentences, or one amazing paragraph, or five hundred inspirational words. Just be prepared for the question and have an answer. Your students will probably be panicked enough with the unstructured nature of the activity, so a length objective will give them some direction.

- **Help kids with writer's block.** Some kids may be totally stalemated by this challenge. That's understandable, but they'll get better with practice. You can make suggestions, but just be careful not to become too potent of a muse. The goal is for them to do the creating.

- **Be patient with yourself and your students.** This transition won't be easy for you or your students, but once they figure out how to ride this literary bike, they'll have no interest in keeping the training wheels.

Engagement is stifled by rigidly detailed writing prompts. Find the courage to turn the writing process over to your students.

HACK

PUSH POLL WITH TWITTER

THE PROBLEM: STUDENT PREFERENCES ARE OFTEN HIDDEN

A PUSH POLL IS a poll with an agenda. A biased media outlet can word questions in a certain way, or prompt the public at a strategic moment, in order to sway opinion. Teacher-generated Twitter polls have an agenda, but it's not sinister. This hack is geared toward using Twitter's cool polling feature to engage.

Some district IT types quake at the thought of unbridled tweeting in their realm. I get it. It's blocked at my school, but that hasn't prevented me from creating student polls and watching joyful participation. When my students want to tweet, they can either switch out of the school's Wi-Fi, or tweet when they go home.

Some students don't have Twitter accounts, but I never make participation mandatory. And, you can always create a physical copy for anyone who'd like to participate but can't. I'm just generating engagement, getting them thinking about my class even when they're not in my room.

THE HACK: CREATE A TWITTER POLL FOR YOUR STUDENTS

Make a class account. This keeps a separation between your personal life and professional life, which is always smart. Making a poll is remarkably easy. Select the tweet icon and then a text box will appear. Below the box, you'll see a few icons. Choose the one that looks like a pie chart, and *bam!* – you're in poll mode. If you need more guidance, watch the brief Hack Learning instructional video in Image 97.1.

Image 97.1

My polls are voluntary, so my challenge is to make them fun. I teach Global Studies to freshmen. We watch movie segments with some of the units, such as:

- For the unit on fascism, we watched a cheesy movie called *The Wave*, about Mr. Ross, a teacher who attempted to convert his class into Nazis.

- For the unit on the Cold War, we watched portions of *13 Days* where Special Assistant to the President Kenneth O'Donnell tries to prevent nuclear war.

- For the unit on independence movements, we watched segments of *Gandhi*.

- For the unit on genocide, we watched hotel manager Paul Rusesabagina work to keep Tutsis from getting slaughtered in *Hotel Rwanda*.

In my poll, I asked which of these gentlemen would make the best dinner guest. Students were all over my poll like a cheap suit. Check out the poll in Image 97.2.

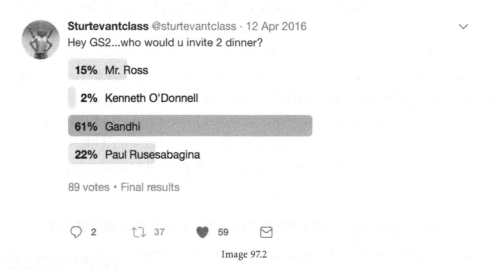

Image 97.2

WHAT YOU CAN DO TOMORROW

- **Create a classroom Twitter account.** This account, separate from your personal account, will be your platform for student preference and expression.

- **Come up with an engaging and fun question.** My question about dinner guests worked because students found it joyful

and intriguing. They said funny things about how each guest would behave, the potential table conversation, and what each guest would like, or demand, to eat.

- **Create a Twitter poll.** Students may, or may not, have the ability to respond in class. Not all of your students will have access to Twitter. Make a physical copy for those kids. Give students at least twenty-four hours to respond.

- **Incentivize participation.** I awarded bonus points for voting, liking, and retweeting. Many students had already voted before they came to my last-period class. That's engagement.

Create a class Twitter account and start polling students. Students will have a blast voicing their opinions.

HACK

USE THE *ENTIRE* SCHOOL BUILDING WITH THIS ENGAGING SCAVENGER HUNT

THE PROBLEM: YOUR NEXT LESSON LOOKS A BIT DRY

As I read through the twenty-page assignment on the Industrial Revolution, I kept thinking to myself, *Wow, this is boring.* If I was feeling that burn, imagine what my students were going to feel. I decided it was time to break out of the box. In this case, literally break out of the box of the four walls of my classroom.

THE HACK: SEND STUDENTS ON A SCHOOL-WIDE SCAVENGER HUNT

If you've ever gone to a pet store and played with penned-up puppies, you get this. You sit in the play area with the canine toddler as it literally bounces off the walls with excitement. What's true for dogs is true for kids. We keep our students penned up all day in confining desks. My old superintendent used to complain about the industrial model of education. She frequently pointed out that we often have to warehouse students. That's a frightening and accurate analogy. This hack will liberate kids and allow them to roam around like freed puppies. They'll be grateful.

Decide what big concepts you want your students to grasp from the lesson. Create a number of prompts that will lead to deep investigation. But the beauty of this hack

Image 98.1

is in the way in which you'll deliver these prompts via a QR Code Scavenger Hunt.

The first ingredient in this engagement recipe is for students to download the i-nigma QR code reader, like you may have done to navigate the codes in this book. The second ingredient is to produce QR codes. Please don't be intimidated by this step. Classroom Tools has a remarkably easy-to-use QR Treasure Hunt Generator. Merely type in the questions and answers, and then Classroom Tools will generate the codes. Point your QR code reader at Image 98.1 to learn how.

You print these codes, and finally, concoct hiding places for the codes around the school building. Create a *Hint List* to help students search. I created ten essential questions from my reading, so I created ten QR codes that led to each prompt. Below is my *Hint List*. I'll bet you could apply many of my hiding places to your building.

Hint List:

1. Finding this one could take you to another level

2. On the back of a warning

3. Where Sturtevant gets his Old-Skool messages

4. These kids looked great in 88

5. Behind something black and gray

6. If you find this one…YOU'RE REALLY ON A ROLL!

7. If you don't find this code, your prospects of winning will be extinguished

8. Open this door and find an awesome relationship

9. If you get to the bottom of where this code is placed…I'll be shocked

10. Search this virtual tool we use daily

ANSWERS:

1. Elevator

2. On the back of the "No Firearms" warning on the front door

3. My mailbox in the main office

4. The Class of 1988 composite

5. On the backside of a trash can in the hallway

6. On the large paper rolls in the supply room

7. On an obscure fire extinguisher

8. On the backside of my wife's office door

9. On the bottom of the defibrillator in the basement

10. On the "About" section of Google Classroom

Image 98.2 will lead to my blog post where my students describe this fun and challenging tactic.

Image 98.2

WHAT YOU CAN DO TOMORROW

- **Create essential questions from your lesson or unit.** I created ten questions, but ten was perhaps too many; they were nowhere near finishing finding the codes and diving into the questions when the period ended. I also allowed kids to work with a partner.

- **Download the i-nigma QR code reader.** Your students must download this too.

- **Create QR codes on Classroom Tools.** Simply build your questions and plug them into the generator.

- **Determine hiding places for codes around the building.** Please feel free to steal my hiding places.

- **Craft a Hint Sheet.** If your hiding spots are tough, like mine were, they'll desperately need this.

Morph a dull lesson into challenging your students to hustle around the building formulating wonderful responses to the day's essential questions.

HACK

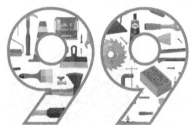

SHOW UP AT YOUR STUDENT'S 30TH BIRTHDAY SURPRISE PARTY

THE PROBLEM: TEACHERS ASSUME THAT STUDENTS KNOW THEIR CLASSMATES

I'LL BET YOU'VE had this experience as a student: You've sat next to a classmate all semester. Then one day, he does a class demonstration for a project. You're shocked to learn that he is a five-star chef, speaks Mandarin, can start a campfire with flint, is related to Denzel Washington, can execute extreme yoga poses, is a sommelier, or is an Olympic plastic cup stacker. All of a sudden, this person becomes vastly more interesting, if not attractive. I'm five foot seven with a shaved head. When I reminisce about my courting days, it's clear that I experienced much more romantic success after some of my classroom demonstrations.

THE HACK: FOSTER STUDENT COLLABORATION WITH A TOTALLY ORIGINAL ICEBREAKER

I change my seating chart after each unit, so I use a lot of icebreakers. My favorites are the ones I invent on the fly. This hack will feature an icebreaker that magically dawned on me on a commute to school one dark and icy February morning. This hastily improvised class activity acted like a ray of May sunshine on a bleak Ohio winter morning. Please give this a try.

Instruct students to subtract their current age from the number thirty. I have a lot of seventeen-year-olds. Their answer is thirteen. Next, tell kids to close their eyes and think about thirteen years in the future. Have them imagine coming home from work on their thirtieth birthday. As they open the door and turn on the lights, they are greeted by a roomful of people yelling, *Surprise!* As the reality comes into focus, they recognize faces from the class they are currently seated in, including your face! Everyone is thirteen years older. How will everyone look? Tell kids to open their eyes.

Project a Google Stopwatch on your smartboard. Inform kids that they have one minute to decide where they're living when we all descend upon them thirteen years in the future. If they don't come up with an answer, they are sentenced to live in their parents' basement. Hopefully, this mild bit of shaming will dissuade them from choosing this stagnant option! After they know where they'll live, students must then consult their devices. Explain that everyone is going to meet here in the classroom and then travel to their new home for their thirtieth surprise birthday party. Have kids plug their future residence into a directions search. They need to calculate the distance between where they are currently sitting, in the classroom, to their future address. Once they have their mileage number, send the class to the hallway. Your door will represent the shortest trip. Students will then sort themselves extending down the hallway. The farther away they'll move away from home, the farther from the door they'll situate themselves.

Image 99.1

Next comes the bonding part. Direct students to lean against the wall. You camp out on the opposing wall facing your kids roughly in the middle of the line. Bring kids up one a time and have them lean against the wall beside you. Have them explain their new location and why they chose it. Kids will learn about their peers' plans and relationships will be forged. And finally, students lined up in this fashion represent a remarkable, random, brand new seating chart. Access Image 99.1 to hear more details about this icebreaker and two other fun ones.

WHAT YOU CAN DO TOMORROW

- **Challenge kids to select a future home location.** This may be challenging for students, but even the unwilling will find the challenge memorable.

- **Direct kids to self-sort in the hallway based on distance from the current location.** I was amazed at how easily kids found their distances. Build your new seating chart based on this random line.

- **Feature students individually.** Call students to the opposite wall. Have them face their peers and explain their future residence choice.

- **Conduct a debriefing.** Ask kids to report something interesting they learned about a classmate.

When kids become more familiar with one another, collaboration follows. Student relationships and collaboration are foundational to engagement.

HACK

MODEL
ENGAGEMENT

THE PROBLEM: MANY TEACHERS ARE FAIRLY ISOLATED

THIS BOOK IS filled with student engagement ideas. Hopefully, you've read some hacks and thought, *I know exactly what I'm doing tomorrow in class!* But, are you an engaged teacher? Educators are often reminded that they must be good role models. It's hard not to look at an educator as a hypocrite. It's tough to take an out-of-shape teacher seriously when he promotes the importance of working out. It's difficult when she complains to students about their cell phone use being a distraction…and then the complaining teacher keeps sneaking peeks at her own phone while the students are preoccupied with an assignment. Or more to the point of this hack, an instructor who constantly promotes student collaboration, but rarely collaborates with colleagues, is not a good role model of collaboration.

Teachers need to be good engagement role models. Being a teacher is strange. You can be so oblivious to everything that happens in the school outside of your classroom. I can be guilty of this! I've been teaching for more than three decades. Ten years ago, I was more involved in the school; I went to most extracurricular activities and had an active social life with colleagues. I'm less involved now, but writing this book has forced me to re-evaluate my posture. Next year, I pledge to be more engaged with my school outside of my little Room 111 sanctuary.

Engagement is not limited to the student-teacher relationship.

A few years back, we had a new superintendent who instituted the Professional Learning Community concept, with the goal of staff collaboration. Departments were to meet weekly and form common assessments and share lesson ideas. The PLC was largely successful and helped force needed interaction. But still…it was an administrative agenda. It was another thing we were being forced to do. I'm proposing that you take the initiative and start your own professional learning community.

THE HACK: MODEL ENGAGEMENT

Two key ingredients in student engagement are self-directed learning and collaboration. These ingredients could easily be applied to teacher engagement as well. Collaborating with colleagues is not only a wonderful way to learn and an example of awesome modeling; it's also good for you. Take the initiative and create a strong social support network. Make this agenda yours! Engage with your colleagues to:

- Learn how to use technology.

- Learn how to engage a difficult student.

- Find a more engaging lesson idea.

- Help a colleague who's struggling.

- Share something funny that just happened in class.

- Share a compliment that a student mentioned about your colleague.

- Congregate at lunch and talk about something besides school.

WHAT YOU CAN DO TOMORROW

- **Compliment a colleague.** Nothing makes a teacher's day more than a heartfelt compliment. In the private sector, bonuses are material. In our realm, we are rewarded with human capital.

- **Do an observation.** It's supremely flattering as a teacher to have a respected colleague approach and say, "I've heard so many awesome things about your class. Would you mind if I sit in tomorrow? I think I could learn a thing or two from you!" Try this tomorrow.

- **Issue an invitation.** Hopefully, you're implementing one of the cool hacks from this book tomorrow in class. If so, how about letting your colleagues know? Compose an email to the staff describing what you're doing and roll out the welcome mat! Don't worry about coming across as self-promotional. Issue a challenge that you'd love for colleagues to follow suit and offer invitations. Perhaps you'll start a movement that will thrill your principal.

- **Ask for help.** Certainly, no one will think you're self-promotional if you compose an email along these lines: *I can't choose between Assignments and Announcements on Google Classroom. Somebody help me.* You'll be amazed at how responsive colleagues can be if you humbly give them the chance.

- **Offer a solution.** Reach out and help a colleague who's struggling. He'll never forget this act of kindness and will return the favor.

Engagement is not limited to the student-teacher relationship. Be a wonderful engagement role model, get answers from colleagues, help colleagues who are struggling, and build a solid social support network in the process.

CONCLUSION

I AM AN OPTIMIST, but I'm also human. Occasionally, I'll get in a bad mood. When I get in such a funk, I become invested in maintaining my crabbiness, but invariably a blessed event undermines my drama.

At the conclusion of my first engagement book, I told a story about my first day of school in 2010. I was bemoaning the news that the State Teachers Retirement System of Ohio had been cratered by the Recession of 2008. The upshot was that all Buckeye public educators would be forced to teach more years than we had planned. This was particularly painful for me because I was approaching retirement and looking forward to a new life chapter. The first day commenced on a murky and muggy August morning. My mood matched the bland overcast sky. I welcomed my new students, but not with my signature enthusiasm. I was struggling. Thankfully, a sweet fourteen-year-old girl greeted me and knocked me off my pity perch by telling me that she was excited to be in my class.

This rather innocent event not only undermined my temporary drama, but it profoundly morphed my paradigm. That incident, which I detail in the previous book, was transformational. It was like a breath of pure oxygen after surfacing from the deep and dark end of the swimming pool. I'm now a born-again educator who raced past my delayed retirement date in early October of 2016, and instead of cashing in my professional chips on that gorgeous autumn day, I instead got excited about exposing my students to Tweetdeck.

After my educational *Come to Jesus* moment, I threw myself back into this noble calling. I was honored to mentor a student teacher. Instead of droning on constantly about lesson plans, he and I decided to focus primarily on relationships. I figured the content and pedagogy part of teaching was easier to master. He was the perfect student teacher for me at the perfect time. He developed an epic academic bedside manner.

When his professor observed him, she was blown away by the classroom culture. When she asked me how I created such a classroom atmosphere, I was perplexed and couldn't put it into words at the time. Her question haunted me to the point that I decided to write a book about it. In the winter of 2014, my first book, *You've Gotta Connect,* hit the shelves. Going from being the guy who was counting the years until retirement, to the guy who just published a book to help other teachers, was like your mama unexpectedly producing your favorite dessert after a leisurely and savory meal. Being an author was not on my bucket list; it just happened. Life can be surprising if you chase a question with passion.

After my book was published, I was invited to appear on a few podcasts. Those interviews exposed me to a virtual social network of like-minded educators. Mark Barnes is the publisher of the *Hack Learning Series*. Mark is part of a Voxer group, and I was invited to join. We quickly became friends. In early 2016, Mark approached me about writing a book on engagement. I embraced the opportunity and spent the first half of 2016 creating *Hacking Engagement*. Near the end of the writing process, Mark and I brainstormed the idea of launching a podcast that mirrored my book. The *Hacking Engagement Podcast* set sail in June that year. Mark and I decided the manuscript should include some QR codes that direct the reader to podcast episodes where hacks are further explored. Thanks to book sales and the growth of the podcast, the laws of supply and demand dictated to Mark and me in early 2017 that more hacks were needed. That's why *Hacking Engagement Again* was hatched.

My paradigm shifted in 2010. Teaching is now enthralling. I have zero plans to retire. What happened to me, could happen to you. Teaching should be a lot of fun. Your students should love stepping into your class. Please don't wish your life away by counting the days until summer vacation, or the years until retirement. Instead of a sweet fourteen-year-old girl extending a compliment, perhaps this book will be your catalyst. Apply one of the fifty recipes from *Hacking Engagement Again* and make tomorrow's lesson delicious. Then build off that success by trying more hacks. By semester's end, your class could become your students' favorite. Good luck engaging your students tomorrow!

OTHER BOOKS IN THE
HACK LEARNING SERIES

HACKING EDUCATION
10 Quick Fixes For Every School

By Mark Barnes (@markbarnes19) & Jennifer Gonzalez (@cultofpedagogy)

In the bestselling *Hacking Education*, Mark Barnes and Jennifer Gonzalez employ decades of teaching experience and hundreds of discussions with education thought leaders to show you how to find and hone the quick fixes that every school and classroom need. Using a Hacker's mentality, they provide **one Aha moment after another** with 10 Quick Fixes For Every School – solutions to everyday problems and teaching methods that any teacher or administrator can implement immediately.

"Barnes and Gonzalez don't just solve problems; they turn teachers into hackers – a transformation that is right on time."

— **DON WETTRICK**, AUTHOR OF *PURE GENIUS*

MAKE WRITING
5 Teaching Strategies That Turn Writer's Workshop Into a Maker Space

By Angela Stockman (@angelastockman)

Everyone's favorite education blogger and writing coach, Angela Stockman, turns teaching strategies and practices upside down in the bestselling, *Make Writing*. She spills you out of your chair, shreds your lined paper, and launches you and your writer's workshop into the maker space! Stockman provides five right-now writing strategies that reinvent instruction and **inspire both young and adult writers** to express ideas with tools that have rarely, if ever, been considered. *Make Writing* is a fast-paced journey inside Stockman's Western New York Young Writer's Studio, alongside the students there who learn how to write and how to make, employing Stockman's unique teaching methods.

"Offering suggestions for using new materials in old ways, thoughtful questions, and specific tips for tinkering and finding new audiences, this refreshing book is inspiring and practical in equal measure."

— AMY LUDWIG VANDERWATER, AUTHOR AND TEACHER

HACKING ASSESSMENT
10 Ways to Go Gradeless in a Traditional Grades School

By Starr Sackstein (@mssackstein)

In the bestselling *Hacking Assessment,* award-winning teacher and world-renowned formative assessment expert Starr Sackstein unravels one of education's oldest mysteries: How to assess learning without grades – even in a school that uses numbers, letters, GPAs, and report cards. While many educators can only muse about the possibility of a world without grades, teachers like Sackstein are **reimagining education**. In this unique, eagerly anticipated book, Sackstein shows you exactly how to create a remarkable no-grades classroom like hers, a vibrant place where students grow, share, thrive, and become independent learners who never ask, "What's this worth?"

"The beauty of the book is that it is not an empty argument against grades – but rather filled with valuable alternatives that are practical and will help to refocus the classroom on what matters most."

— ADAM BELLOW, WHITE HOUSE PRESIDENTIAL INNOVATION FELLOW

HACKING THE COMMON CORE
10 Strategies for Amazing Learning in a Standardized World

By Michael Fisher (@fisher1000)

In *Hacking the Common Core,* longtime teacher and CCSS specialist Mike Fisher shows you how to bring fun back to learning, with ten amazing hacks for teaching all core subjects, while engaging students and making learning fun. Fisher's experience and insights help teachers and parents better understand close reading, balancing fiction and nonfiction, using projects with the core and much more. *Hacking the Common Core* provides **read-tonight-implement-tomorrow strategies** for teaching the standards in fun and engaging ways, improving teaching and learning for students, parents, and educators.

HACKING LEADERSHIP
10 Ways Great Leaders Inspire Learning That Teachers, Students, and Parents Love

By Joe Sanfelippo (@joesanfelippoFC) and Tony Sinanis (@tonysinanis)

In the runaway bestseller *Hacking Leadership*, renowned school leaders Joe Sanfelippo and Tony Sinanis bring readers inside schools that few stakeholders have ever seen – places where students not only come first but have a unique voice in teaching and learning. Sanfelippo and Sinanis ignore the bureaucracy that stifles many leaders, focusing instead on building a culture of **engagement, transparency, and most important, fun**. *Hacking Leadership* has superintendents, principals, and teacher leaders around the world employing strategies they never before believed possible.

"The authors do a beautiful job of helping leaders focus inward, instead of outward. This is an essential read for leaders who are, or want to lead, learner-centered schools."
— GEORGE COUROS, AUTHOR OF *THE INNOVATOR'S MINDSET*

HACKING LITERACY
5 Ways To Turn Any Classroom Into a Culture Of Readers

By Gerard Dawson (@gerarddawson3)

In *Hacking Literacy*, classroom teacher, author, and reading consultant Gerard Dawson reveals five simple ways any educator or parent can turn even the most reluctant reader into a thriving, enthusiastic lover of books. Dawson cuts through outdated pedagogy and standardization, turning reading theory into practice, sharing **valuable reading strategies**, and providing what *Hack Learning Series* readers have come to expect – actionable, do-it-tomorrow strategies that can be built into long-term solutions.

HACKING ENGAGEMENT
50 Tips & Tools to Engage Teachers and Learners Daily

By James Alan Sturtevant (@jamessturtevant)

Some students hate your class. Others are just bored. Many are too nice, or too afraid, to say anything about it. Don't let it bother you; it happens to the best of us. But now, it's **time to engage!** In *Hacking Engagement*, the seventh book in the *Hack Learning Series*, veteran high school teacher, author, and popular podcaster James Sturtevant provides 50 – that's right five-oh – tips and tools that will engage even the most reluctant learners daily.

HACKING HOMEWORK
10 Strategies That Inspire Learning Outside the Classroom

By Starr Sackstein (@mssackstein) and Connie Hamilton (@conniehamilton)

Learning outside the classroom is being reimagined, and student engagement is better than ever. World-renowned author/educator Starr Sackstein has changed how teachers around the world look at traditional grades. Now she's teaming with veteran educator, curriculum director, and national presenter Connie Hamilton to bring you **ten powerful strategies** for teachers and parents that promise to inspire independent learning at home, without punishments or low grades.

"Starr Sackstein and Connie Hamilton have assembled a book full of great answers to the question, 'How can we make homework engaging and meaningful?'"

— **DOUG FISHER & NANCY FREY**, AUTHORS/PRESENTERS

HACKING PROJECT BASED LEARNING
10 Easy Steps to PBL and Inquiry in the Classroom

By Ross Cooper (@rosscoops31) and Erin Murphy (@murphysmusings5)

As questions and mysteries around PBL and inquiry continue to swirl, experienced classroom teachers and school administrators Ross Cooper and Erin Murphy have written a book that will empower those intimidated by PBL to cry, "I can do this!" while at the same time providing added value for those who are already familiar with the process. *Hacking Project Based*

Learning demystifies what PBL is all about with **ten hacks that construct a simple path** that educators and students can easily follow to achieve success.

"*Hacking Project Based Learning* is a classroom essential. Its ten simple 'hacks' will guide you through the process of setting up a learning environment in which students will thrive from start to finish."

— Daniel H. Pink, New York Times Bestselling Author of *DRIVE*

HACK LEARNING ANTHOLOGY
Innovative Solutions for Teachers and Leaders

Edited by Mark Barnes (@markbarnes19)

Anthology brings you the most innovative education hacks from the first nine books in the *Hack Learning Series*. Written by twelve award-winning classroom teachers, principals, superintendents, college instructors, and international presenters, *Anthology* is every educator's new problem-solving handbook. It is both a preview of nine other books and a **full-fledged, feature-length blueprint** for solving your biggest school and classroom problems.

HACKING GOOGLE FOR EDUCATION
99 Ways to Leverage Google Tools in Classrooms, Schools, and Districts

By Brad Currie (@bradmcurrie), Billy Krakower (@wkrakower), and Scott Rocco (@ScottRRocco)

If you could do more with Google than search, what would it be? Would you use Google Hangouts to connect students to cultures around the world? Would you finally achieve a paperless workflow with Classroom? Would you inform and engage stakeholders district-wide through Blogger? Now, you can say Yes to all of these, because Currie, Krakower, and Rocco remove the limits in Hacking Google for Education, giving you **99 Hacks in 33 chapters**, covering Google in a unique way that benefits all stakeholders.

"Connected educators have long sought a comprehensive resource for implementing blended learning with G Suite. Hacking Google for Education superbly delivers with a plethora of classroom-ready solutions and linked exemplars."

— Dr. Robert R. Zywicki, Superintendent of Weehawken Township School District

HACK LEARNING RESOURCES

All Things Hack Learning:

hacklearning.org

The Entire Hack Learning Series on Amazon:

hacklearningbooks.com

The Hack Learning Podcast, Hosted by Mark Barnes:

hacklearningpodcast.com

The Hacking Engagement Podcast, Hosted by James Sturtevant:

jamesalansturtevant.com

Hack Learning on Twitter:

@HackMyLearning

#HackLearning

#HackingLeadership

#HackingLiteracy

#HackingEngagement

#HackingHomework

#HackingPBL

#MakeWriting

#HackGoogleEdu

#EdTechMissions

#ParentMantras

#MovieTeacher

Hack Learning on Facebook:

facebook.com/hacklearningseries

Hack Learning on Instagram:

hackmylearning

The Hack Learning Academy:

hacklearningacademy.com

MEET THE AUTHOR

 **James Alan Sturtevant** has taught in Delaware County, in Central Ohio, for over three decades. His first book, *You've Gotta Connect*, details how teachers can build essential relationships with students. He has appeared on many popular podcasts and authored guest posts on *Edutopia*, the *Huffington Post*, and *Principal Leadership*. Sturtevant remains committed to helping teachers forge strong relationships with kids, but his true passion is student engagement. With his *Hacking Engagement Podcast* and books, he helps educators create classrooms and schools that captivate kids and empower them to learn.

ACKNOWLEDGEMENTS

I WOULD LIKE TO thank my friend and publisher Mark Barnes. This book was conceptualized and then created as a result of our many casual and thoroughly enjoyable conversations. I'd like to acknowledge all of my amazing educational comrades who enriched the pages of *Hacking Engagement Again* with their brilliance. And finally, I owe my largest debt of gratitude to my clan. Thank you, Jason, Niki, David, Maria, Kaia, little Myles, and Penny, my life partner and biggest supporter.

PUBLICATIONS

Times 10 is helping all education stakeholders improve every aspect of teaching and learning. We are committed to solving big problems with simple ideas. We bring you content from experts, shared through multiple channels, including books, podcasts, and an array of social networks. Our mantra is simple: Read it today; fix it tomorrow. Stay in touch with us at HackLearning.org, at hashtag #HackLearning on Twitter, and on the Hack Learning Facebook group.

Made in the USA
Monee, IL
22 January 2020